POETRY NOW

LEAVING CERTIFICATE
ENGLISH POETRY
ORDINARY LEVEL 2013

Edited by

Niall MacMonagle

The Celtic Press

' . . . until everything
was rainbow, rainbow, rainbow!'

Elizabeth Bishop

First published in 2011 by The Celtic Press
Unit 16, Goldenbridge Industrial Estate, Dublin 8.

Introduction, Notes and Critical Apparatus
Copyright © Niall MacMonagle 2011

Design and Layout Raven Design
Printed in Ireland by ColourBooks Ltd.

ISBN 978–1–907705–11-3

Contents

Introduction 1
How to use this book 11

Part I
Prescribed Poems at Ordinary Level 12

For Heidi with Blue Hair	*Fleur Adcock* 14
The Hug	*Tess Gallagher* 18
Daniel's Duck	*Kerry Hardie* 23
Night Drive	*Brendan Kennelly* 29
Badger	*Michael Longley* 36
When I consider how my light is spent'	*John Milton* 42
Anseo	*Paul Muldoon* 47
Problems	*Julie O'Callaghan* 53
The Sun	*Mary Oliver* 57
Will we work together?	*Marge Piercy* 62
Jungian Cows	*Penelope Shuttle* 67
Madly Singing in the City	*Peter Sirr* 72
Traveling through the Dark	*William Stafford* 77
Do Not Go Gentle Into That Good Night	*Dylan Thomas* 81
Chronicle	*David Wheatley* 86
A Summer Morning	*Richard Wilbur* 91

Part II
Prescribed Poets at Ordinary Level 96

Elizabeth Bishop (1911 – 1979) 98
The Fish 100
The Prodigal 109
Filling Station 114

Gerard Manley Hopkins (1844 – 1889) 118
Spring 120
Inversnaid 125

Thomas Kinsella (Born 1928) 130
Thinking of Mr D 132
Mirror in February 135

Derek Mahon (b. 1941) 140
Grandfather 142
After the Titanic 144
Antarctica 147

Sylvia Plath (1932 – 1963) 152
Poppies in July (1962) 154
The Arrival of the Bee Box (1962) 157
Child (1963) 161

Adrienne Rich (B. 1929) 164
Aunt Jennifer's Tigers 166
The Uncle Speaks in the Drawing Room 169

William Shakespeare (1564 – 1616) 172
'Shall I compare thee to a summer's day?' (18) 174
'Like as the waves make towards the pebbled shore' (60) 178

William Wordsworth (1770 – 1850) 182
'She dwelt among the untrodden ways' 185
'It is a beauteous evening calm and free' 187
from The Prelude Book I – Skating 191

Part III
The Unseen Poem 196

The Poem on the Page 197
The Shape of the Poem on the Page 197
The Unseen Poem – A Response 204
A selection of poems suited to the Unseen Poetry
question at Ordinary Level 207

July Day Spectacular	*Nornan MacCaig*	209
Eily Kilbride	*Brendan Kennelly*	210
Did Anything Happen at the Field Today, Dear	*Richard Hill*	211
Pot Roast	*Mark Strand*	212
Running on Empty	*Robert Philips*	214
The Jaguar	*Ted Hughes*	216
Over and Over	*Elizabeth Jennings*	217

Part IV
Appendix I
Responding to a poem 220
Appendix II
Two poems by William Carlos Williams 221

A Glossary of Literary Terms 222
Acknowledgements 233

Introduction

"Study is the resting place – poetry the adventure'
Wallace Stevens

The Leaving Certificate student is already an experienced reader of poetry. For Junior Certificate you were invited to read a great variety of poems on a wide range of subjects by many different poets and a similiar challenge awaits the student at Leaving Certificate. You will have realised that the poets use language differently, that poetry is both challenging and rewarding and in an age of soundbites and mediaspeak it can hold its own and offer something unique and special; that poetry, in Allison Pearson's words, 'is not in the business of taking polaroids: it should be a long slow developer, raising images that we frame and keep'.

The American poet Mary Oliver says that 'Poetry is a river; many voices travel in it; poem after poem moves along in the exciting crests and falls of the river waves. None is timeless; each arrives in an historical context; almost everything, in the end passes. But the desire to make a poem, and the world's willingness to receive it – indeed the world's need of it – these never pass.'

It is worth remembering at the outset that the word for poet in English comes from the Greek word for maker. A good poem is language that has been carefully shaped and well made. Samuel Taylor Coleridge's definition of poetry in the nineteenth century as 'the best words in the best order' still holds. W. H. Auden has described poetry as 'memorable speech'; the American critic Helen Vendler says 'Poetry is the most speaking of written signs; it is the most designed of spoken utterances.' The New Princeton Handbook of Poetic Terms defines a poem as 'an instance of verbal art, a text set in verse, bound speech. More generally, a poem conveys heightened forms of perception, experience, meaning, or consciousness in heightened language, i.e., a heightened mode of discourse.' But whichever definition we use, we will find definitions inadequate and less important than the unique and individual experience which is ours when we, as readers, allow ourselves to enter into the world of the poem which the poet has created for us on the page.

'The Voice You Hear When You Read Silently' by Thomas Lux reminds us of the unique, very private, pleasurable experience of reading poetry:

The Voice You Hear When You Read Silently

is not silent, it is a speaking–
out-loud voice in your head: it is spoken,
a voice is saying it
as you read. It's the writer's words,
of course, in a literary sense
his or her 'voice' but the sound
of that voice is the sound of your voice.
Not the sound your friends know
or the sound of a tape played back
but your voice
caught in the dark cathedral
of your skull, your voice heard
by an internal ear informed by internal abstracts
and what you know by feeling,
having felt. It is your voice
saying, for example, the word 'barn'
that the writer wrote
but the 'barn' you say
is a barn you know or knew. The voice
in your head, speaking as you read,
never says anything neutrally – some people
hated the barn they knew,
some people love the barn they know
so you hear the word loaded
and a sensory constellation
is lit: horse-gnawed stalls,
hayloft, black heat tape wrapping
a water pipe, a slippery
spilled chirrr of oats from a split sack,
the bony, filthy haunches of cows . . .
And 'barn' is only a noun – no verb
or subject has entered into the sentence yet!
The voice you hear when you read to yourself
is the clearest voice: you speak it
speaking to you.

•

When we look at a poem, any poem, for the very first time we can
appreciate and sense how that poem has been made and shaped. This
does not only include its actual shape as printed text, though this in itself
is extremely important; more importantly, it means that thought, idea,
and feeling have been structured and the careful combination produces
the living poem.

An open approach brings its own rewards. If we come to understand how something complex works, then we are aware of its intricacies and we can better admire the creative mind that made it possible. Michael Longley says that 'a poet makes the most complex and concentrated response that can be made with words to the total experience of living.' But he also admits that one of the things which studying literature taught him was 'the beauty of things difficult.'

It is an exciting challenge to stand before a painting and discover what it has to say to us, to listen to a piece of music and hear it for the first time, to read a poem unknown to us until that moment. And then to return to these works and to realise how our relationship with them changes and develops as we ourselves change and develop. As we grow and change, so does our response. Every encounter with a work of art is an encounter with individuality and in this way we as individuals understand ourselves and others more. Let the poems in this book have their say and you will not be disappointed.

We can all remember instances and experiences which we found difficult and challenging initially but, with careful thought and an open, positive approach, we gained insight and understanding. You will know this already from your Junior Certificate. Stephen Booth puts it like this: 'Any reader superstitiously fearful that the magic of a poem will vanish with knowledge of its sources need not worry any more than a student of zoology need worry that gazelles will slow down if he investigates the reasons why they run so fast.' Helen Vendler offers good advice when she says that a reader should not look at a poem 'as if you're looking at the text with a microscope from outside'. For Vendler, the close reader is 'someone who goes inside a room and describes the architecture. You speak from inside the poem as someone looking to see how the roof articulates with the walls and how the wall articulates with the floor. And where are the crossbeams that hold it up, and where are the windows that let light through?'

Reject challenge and we stagnate. If we did reject challenge our vocabulary, for example, would never grow; the enquiring mind would close down. Sometimes we fall into the trap of saying 'I like this poem because it is easy for me to understand' or the equally dangerous and unsatisfactory response: 'Why doesn't the poet say what he or she wants to say in an easy-to-understand language?' If we adopt such a view we are saying that we want a poetry that is at our level only, that if there is an unknown word or an allusion then the poem should be rejected. If we spoke down to little children throughout their childhood they would never grow up. Most poetry is written by adults for other adults and, as a Leaving Certificate student, you are on the threshold of adulthood. If you do come upon a poem in a newspaper, magazine, book, the London

Underground, the New York Subway or the DART, you should give that poem a chance. The poem deserves it, and so do you.

•

Some years back the poet Paul Muldoon was asked to judge a poetry competition, in the North of Ireland, which was open to young people up to the age of eighteen. There were hundreds of entries and there were poems, short and long, on all the big subjects – famine, time, death, space travel, nuclear war. Muldoon awarded first prize to an eight-year old boy who wrote the following poem:

The Tortoise

The tortoise goes movey, movey.

There was 'consternation' when 'this little poem about a tiny little subject' was awarded the prize and Muldoon explains that a great deal of the consternation was in the minds of the schoolteachers in the audience. They were upset by the fact that there's no such word in the English language as "movey, m-o-v-e-y". I tried to point out that until recently that there'd been no such word as "movey", but there now certainly was such a word, and I would never again be able to think of a tortoise without seeing it go "movey, movey".' One teacher told Muldoon that the prize- winning poet was illiterate, forgetting that the same boy had an extraordinary fresh and alive imagination.

Consider the poem again. Say it aloud and its atmospheric rhythm is immediate:

The Tortoise

The tortoise goes movey, movey.

Professor Paul Muldoon now teaches creative writing at Princeton and the first task he sets his students is to write a one-line poem that will change the way he looks at the world. When they have made their poem, he shows them 'The Tortoise', which, for him, does just that. It goes m-o-v-e-y, m-o-v-e-y.

•

There are many aspects to be considered when it comes to the poem on the page, but let us begin without any set ideas. Consider the following:

In a Station of the Metro

The apparition of these faces in the crowd;
Petals on a wet, black bough.

Ezra Pound (1885 – 1972)

What have we here? A poem. How can we tell? One of the reasons we can identify it as poetry is by its very arrangement on the page. Prose is presented within a right and left hand margin on the page, whereas poetry is written in lines, each one causing us to pause, however briefly, before we move on. When we read it through we can sense a concentration and intensity, a focus, a way of looking, which is one of poetry's hallmarks. What have we here? Three lines, the first of them the title, then two lines separated by a semi-colon; twenty words in all. For accurate understanding almost all you need is a dictionary: remember Elizabeth Bishop's advice: 'Use the dictionary. It's better than the critics'.

To ask 'What have we here?' is infinitely more rewarding than 'What is this poem about?' And this, I think, is by far the best way of approaching any text. 'What have I here?' means that I, in my own time, will interpret the poem. I will gradually build up an understanding of it in my own mind. A poem is not a static thing. It is, in Thomas Kinsella's words, 'an orderly dynamic entity'. 'What is this poem about?' is an alienating way of looking at a text, implying as it does that there is only one way of looking at the poem and that I, as reader, must somehow crack some code. We all bring different things to a text. My way of looking at a poem will be different from yours. The person who has caught a fish will read Elizabeth Bishop's poem 'The Fish' in a different light from the reader who has never held a fishing rod. If you have dyed your hair blue against the wishes of the school authorities then Fleur Adcock's poem 'For Heidi with Blue Hair' will hold particular resonances. Similarly if you have grown up on a farm you may find yourself reading Seamus Heaney's poetry from a different perspective to the urban dweller. One way is not necessarily better than the other. It is different. What does matter, however, is that interpretation and discussion of the text should be rooted in the text itself. There is such a thing as a wrong interpretation: one which does not take the details of the text into account.

•

In the short poem by Ezra Pound the title 'In a Station of the Metro' gives us the setting of the poem.

In a Station of the Metro

The apparition of these faces in the crowd;
Petals on a wet, black bough.

We are in Paris, but the actual Metro stop is not named. The title is factual; there is no word in the title to indicate an attitude, a tone. Yet the reader is immediately invited to imagine this particular scene: usually a crowded and very busy underground railway station. In many ways it is a scene that sums up an aspect of twentieth-century life – urban, anonymous, busy, lacking individuality.

Then the first line of the poem itself speaks of the individual and separate faces in the crowd. Pound, on seeing particular faces, compares the experience to that of experiencing an apparition. The faces are somehow supernatural or ghostly. In a world of concrete and steel the human being is phantom-like. This is a sense impression. The poem, for example, has no verb. It is not so much concerned with making a definite statement as with capturing an immediate response to a situation at a particular moment in time.

The second and final line of the poem speaks about the natural world, petals on a tree. The tree itself is wet and black suggesting, perhaps, something unattractive; but the petals are wet too and therefore shiny. They stand out. There are many of them and yet each one is individual and unique. From the way the two lines are arranged on the page and the use of the connecting semi-colon, we can tell that Pound is obviously making a connection between the nameless faces of people moving through an underground station with their bright faces and the petals that stand out against the dull tree bough.

The train in the underground station is a hard, steel object and, it could be argued, bough-like in shape. The faces coming towards Pound are soft, living faces; the petals are soft against the hard surface of the tree, just as the faces are bright against the background of the Metro.

Ezra Pound has defined an image as 'an intellectual and emotional complex in an instant of time' and you can see how this poem is such an image. It captures the idea and the feeling, the intellectual and the emotional, and both are linked together within the one picture.

Pound himself has written of how he came to write this poem. He left the Metro at La Concorde and 'saw suddenly a beautiful face, and then another beautiful woman, and I tried all that day to find words for what this had meant to me, and I could not find any words that seemed to me worthy, or as lovely as that sudden emotion.' Later he wrote a thirty-line poem and destroyed it. Six months after that he wrote a poem half that length; a year later he made the haiku-like poem 'In a Station of the Metro'.

The above observations on this poem are far longer than the poem itself, but poetry is compression and intensity. So much is being said in such a short space that any discussion of a poem will require expansion and explanation. What is most important of all is that you feel comfortable and at ease with poetry. You speak the language in which it is written and this allows us to be closer to poetry and literature than any other art form; the words are ours already or, as we read, they become ours, as well as the poet's. There may be no one single, definitive response, explanation or interpretation to a poem, but there are wrongheaded ones. Take care and then the private dialogue between you and the poem, the class discussion and the personal study of the text become a very rewarding and enriching experience.

•

The philosophy behind this Leaving Certificate English Course is 'knowledge made, not knowledge received.' In other words you are expected to take an active, not a passive, part in the learning process. The knowledge, insight and understanding gained by you is more enjoyable and memorable than the knowledge presented to you by another. That is to say that if we had the time and inclination a library of books would educate us well, if we were willing and enthusiastic readers. However, reality is otherwise. Most of us find a system and a structure, such as classroom and school, necessary, if not vital – initially at any rate. So we go to school and find ourselves in English class studying poems and poets and poetry.

Each year young people worldwide study poetry in school. It is an art form that exists in every known language. It is also known that only a small percentage of people continue to read poetry throughout their adult life, despite the fact that many enjoy it and remember it from school. This is changing, however. Poetry readings now attract very large audiences; in Ireland Poetry Ireland administers a Writers-in-School scheme whereby a writer can visit a school and read from and discuss his or her work; more poetry books are being sold; occasionally, poetry books even become best-sellers. Birthday Letters by Ted Hughes, for example, sold over 120,000 copies in one year and 200,000 hardback copies of Seamus Heaney's translation of Beowulf were bought in 2000.

•

Silence and slow time are not things that we associate with the way we live today. Yet silence and slow time are probably the two most important things when it comes to the intensely private experience of reading poetry. There are specifically public poems as well, of course. Britain's Poet Laureate celebrates moments of national significance; Bill Clinton had the African-American poet Maya Angelou read her specially commissioned poem 'On The Pulse Of Morning ' at his Inauguration in 1993; when President Mary McAleese was inaugurated she quoted from Christopher Logue's poem 'Come to the Edge'. On 11 November 2004 in her Re-Inaugural speech President McAleese ended with a quotation from a poem by Seamus Heaney, a poem which had been written especially to mark the expansion, six months earlier, of the European Union on 1 May: 'Move lips, move minds and make new meanings flare'.

And in the wake of the attacks on America on 11 September 2001, people turned to poetry in great numbers. Walt Whitman's 'Song of Myself', though first published in 1855, seems to capture the recent, unforgettable horror when it speaks of a trapped fireman:

> Tumbling walls buried me in their debris,
> Heat and smoke I inspired, I heard the
>   yelling shouts of my comrades,
> I heard the distant click of their picks and shovels . . . .

or Emily Dickinson's 'After great pain, a formal feeling comes', written circa 1862, ends:

> This is the Hour of Lead —
> Remembered, if outlived,
> As Freezing persons, recollect the Snow —
> First — Chill — then Stupor — then the letting go —

Richard Bernstein, in The New York Times, 13 September 2001, says that in those lines by Dickinson, 'It is the union of experience, insight and the simple beauty of language that helps us to give our own grief a name, that gives us a kind of company, that extends a wise hand' and adds that 'There is no salve to be found in literature before those stricken with tragedy are ready for contemplation. But when that moment comes there is a great richness to be discovered.'

People also turned to Robert Frost and to W.H. Auden, whose poem '1 September 1939' speaks of the uncertainty and fear at the outbreak of World War II and includes the lines:

> Waves of anger and fear
> Circulate over the bright

And darkened lands of the earth,
Obsessing our private lives;
The unmentionable odour of death
Offends the September night.

Poetry does not offer easy answers or solutions but it does allow us to experience emotions. It does not lessen our fear and confusions and anger but it helps us to accept our anger, confusions and fears, and, in Bernstein's words, we find in literature 'a difficult sort of comfort' because great literature 'refuses to provide comfort that is 'false' or 'saccharine'.

•

In the film Invictus, Nelson Mandela, played by Morgan Freeman, tells the Captain of the Springboks rugby team Francois Pienaar that his favourite poem is William Ernest Henley's 'Invictus'. When one remembers that Mandela was imprisoned for twenty-seven years for opposing apartheid, eighteen of which were spent on Robben Island, it is easy to see why such a poem sustained him during his imprisonment:

Invictus

Out of the night that covers me,
Black as the Pit from pole to pole,
I thank whatever gods may be
For my unconquerable soul.

In the fell clutch of circumstance
I have not winced nor cried aloud.
Under the bludgeonings of chance
My head is bloody but unbowed.

Beyond this place of wrath and tears
Looms but the horror of the shade,
And yet the menace of the years
Finds, and shall find me, unafraid.

It matters not how strait the gate,
How charged with punishments the scroll,
I am the master of my fate:
I am the captain of my soul.

William Ernest Henley (1849-1903)

•

This book provides you with the texts, the most important things of all. You may find the critical apparatus of some use, but nothing can replace the lively, engaged, discursive atmosphere in a classroom where poems and poets are discussed between teacher and student and student and student, or the careful reading of the poems and thinking done by you in private. It is hoped that you will return again and again to these wonderful poems and that, long after you have left school, a poet's way of seeing, a poet's way of saying will remain with you for the rest of your life. In an age such as ours, where we often demand and expect instant gratification, the reading and re-reading of poetry is often viewed as an unusual and strange activity. It is also one of the most valuable, enriching and stimulating things you could do. And it can be, as Wallace Stevens reminds us, an adventure.

Niall MacMonagle

How to Use This Book

There are two compulsory poetry questions on Paper II of the Leaving Certificate English course at Ordinary Level: one on the Prescribed Poetry and one on an Unseen Poem. The question on the prescribed poets will be in two parts: one question on the poets who are represented by one poem; one question on the eight poets who are represented by more than one poem and who also feature at Higher Level. The texts will be printed on the examination paper and within each question there will be choices.

Begin with the prescribed poems and read the poems closely, preferably aloud. Then read the poems again (with the aid of the dictionary or glossary if necessary). Think about the poems and talk about the poems. Re-read the poems until you feel comfortable with them. There is no substitute for knowing the poems well; reading the poems and thinking about the poems is the most important of all. The questions beneath each poem will direct you towards some important aspects of the text. Later you may wish to read the Critical Commentary. These may help clarify your own thinking. Finally you should find writing on the texts a very good way of finding out how much you understand.

For the Unseen Poetry question you may find the response to 'A Blessing' by James Wright of interest. There is also an Appendix which includes an outline of various strategies when responding to any poem and a Glossary of Literary Terms.

[American spelling has been retained where appropriate.]

PART I
PRESCRIBED
POEMS

Fleur Adcock (b.1934)

Fleur Adcock was born on 10 February 1934, in Auckland, New Zealand, but lived in England as a child, where she attended eleven different schools: 'We moved around a lot . . . and each time I didn't have any friends so I retreated to an interior world.' In 1947 she returned to New Zealand, attended university there, married at eighteen, had two sons and got divorced at twenty-four. She settled in London in 1963, where she has worked as a librarian and later as a free-lance writer. Adcock has published several collections, including *The Scenic Route* (1974), *The Inner Harbour* (1979), *The Incident Book* (1986) – from which 'For Heidi with Blue Hair' is taken – *Time-Zones* (1991) and *Looking Back* (1997). *Poems 1960 – 2000* is also available. She received an OBE in 1996 and the Queen's Gold Medal for Poetry in 2006. Her most recent collection is *Dragon Talk* [2010].

For Heidi with Blue Hair

When you dyed your hair blue
(or, at least, ultramarine
for the clipped sides, with a crest
of jet-black spikes on top)
you were sent home from school   5

because, as the headmistress put it,
although dyed hair was not
specifically forbidden, yours,
was, apart from anything else,
not done in the school colours.   10

Tears in the kitchen, telephone-calls
to school from your freedom-loving father:
'She's not a punk in her behaviour;
it's just a style.' (You wiped your eyes,
also not in a school colour.)   15

'She discussed it with me first —
we checked the rules.' 'And anyway, Dad,
it cost twenty-five dollars.
Tell them it won't wash out —
not even if I wanted to try.'   20

It would have been unfair to mention
your mother's death, but that
shimmered behind the arguments.
The school had nothing else against you;
the teachers twittered and gave in.   25

Next day your black friend had hers done
in grey, white and flaxen yellow —
the school colours precisely:
an act of solidarity, a witty
tease. The battle was already won.   30

Glossary

2 *ultramarine:* a deep blue. [The word literally means 'beyond' (Latin, *ultra*) 'marine' (*marinus*) – beyond the sea – and this deep-blue pigment was originally made from lapis-lazuli which was rare and brought from a land beyond the sea.]
18 *twenty-five dollars:* New Zealand dollars
29 *solidarity:* holding together, expressing the same interests and aims

Questions

1. Who is speaking in this poem? Identify the different voices. What is the attitude of the aunt towards the hair-dyeing episode? Does it surprise you?

2. What vivid pictures appear in your mind as you read through the poem?

3. What kind of a girl is Fleur Adcock's niece? What kind of a home does she come from? Is the girl's background significant? Does Fleur Adcock think so?

4. What is your feeling when you read the final stanza? Is it the same feeling as the aunt's feeling?

5. This poem tells a story. What differences are there between the story if it were told in prose and this poem version by Adcock?

6. Look at the length of the sentences in this poem. Why do you think the final one is the shortest?

Critical Commentary

The speaker in this poem is Fleur Adcock, aunt, and she is speaking to her niece Heidi, the 'you' of the poem. In a single sentence, the first two stanzas describe in a very straightforward, matter-of-fact way the details of the incident. The bracket contains the most vivid use of language – 'clipped sides', 'crest of jet-black spikes'. The voice of the headmistress is also heard – 'although dyed hair was not specifically forbidden. . .'. There is a humour and humanity in the headmistress's explanation: 'yours was, apart from anything else, not done in the school colours.'

The third and fourth stanzas move from school to home. Adcock brings us to Heidi's kitchen, where she is crying; her father is on the phone to the headmistress, defending his daughter's action. Fleur Adcock adds her own comment in a bracket: (You wiped your eyes,/ also not in a school colour). Such a detail reveals that the poet is gently mocking the headmistress for saying that Heidi's hair wasn't dyed the school colours.

The father is 'freedom-loving', but he also tells the headmistress that he checked the school rules before his daughter dyed her hair.

Heidi, though tearful, is also practical. She mentions how much it cost her to dye her hair – 'twenty-five dollars' – and that it won't wash out. The fact that she says 'not even if I wanted to try' suggests her strong-willed nature.

Another layer of emotion is revealed in stanza five. Heidi's mother is dead, her father seems to be bringing his daughter up alone, but, as Adcock points out, neither mentions this fact to the school authorities. The fact that they don't is a tribute to them both, but the phrase 'shimmered behind the arguments' is an imaginative way of saying how everyone concerned was aware of Heidi's loss and loneliness.

A line such as 'the teachers twittered and gave in' leaves the reader in no doubt as to which side Adcock herself in on. The word 'twittered' and the alliteration on 'teachers twittered' puts them in their place.

The final stanza is positive and upbeat. There is the defiance of the friend's dyed hair, but there is also the clever, humorous gesture of 'grey, white and flaxen yellow —/ the school colours precisely'. The short, last sentence of the poem suggests a small triumph for Heidi, her schoolfriend and school pupils everywhere – a small triumph, but victory nevertheless.

Tess Gallagher (b.1943)

Tess Gallagher was born in 1943 in Port Angeles, Washington and studied at the University of Washington [where she was taught creative writing by the poet Theodore Roethke] and the University of Iowa. Gallagher says that writing poems is like fishing: the people and circumstances of her life are bait. She has said that she writes poems that resemble the little prayers she sent out as a child, for fish to bite. Salmon fishing with her father, she recalls how 'I used to lean out over the water and try to look past my own face, past the reflection of the boat, past the sun and the darkness, down to where the fish were truly swimming. I made up charm songs and word-hopes to tempt the fish.' She married three times and her third husband was the writer Raymond Carver who died in 1988. Her first book, *Stepping Outside*, was published in 1974. *My Black Horse New & Selected Poems* was published in 1995. The San Francisco Chronicle says that 'Gallagher acknowledges loneliness and loss but reaches always for connection.' She chose the words of St Teresa as an epigraph to My Black Horse: 'Words lead to deeds . . . . They prepare the soul, make it ready and move it to tenderness.' Tess Gallagher frequently visits Ireland. A poem from her 1978 collection *Under Stars* is called 'Still Moment at Dun Laoghaire' and 'The Hug' is from *Willingly* [1984]

The Hug

A woman is reading a poem on the street
and another woman stops to listen. We stop too,
with our arms around each other. The poem
is being read and listened to out here
in the open. Behind us   5
no one is entering or leaving the houses.

Suddenly a hug comes over me and I'm
giving it to you, like a variable star shooting light
off to make itself comfortable, then
subsiding. I finish but keep on holding   10
you. A man walks up to us and we know he hasn't
come out of nowhere, but if he could, he
would have. He looks homeless because of how
he needs. 'Can I have one of those?' he asks you,
and I feel you nod. I'm surprised,   15
surprised you don't tell him how
it is – that I'm yours, only
yours, etc., exclusive as a nose to
its face. Love – that's what we're talking about, love
that nabs you with 'for me   20
only' and holds on.

So I walk over to him and put my
arms around him and try to
hug him like I mean it. He's got an overcoat on
so thick I can feel   25
him past it. I'm starting the hug
and thinking, 'How big a hug is this supposed to be?
How long shall I hold this hug?' Already
we could be eternal, his arms falling over my
shoulders, my hands not   30
meeting behind his back, he is so big!

I put my head into his chest and snuggle
in. I lean into him. He stands for it. This is his
and he's starting to give it back so well I know he's
getting it. This hug. So truly, so tenderly   35

we stop having arms and I don't know if
my lover has walked away or what, or
if the woman is still reading the poem, or the houses –
what about them? – the houses.

Clearly, a little permission is a dangerous thing.   40
But when you hug someone you want it
to be a masterpiece of connection, the way the button
on his coat will leave the imprint of
a planet on my cheek
when I walk away.   45
When I try to find some place
to go back to.

Glossary

8 variable: inconsistent, liable to change
10 subsiding: becoming less intense
18 etc: et cetera [Latin] meaning 'and so on'
29 eternal: lasting forever
41 a little permission is a dangerous thing: echoing, perhaps, a well-known
line from Alexander Pope's [1688-1744] poem 'An Essay on Criticism'
[1711]: 'a little learning is a dangerous thing'

Questions

1. Tess Gallagher, in 'My Father's Love Letters,' an Introduction to *My Black Horse New & Selected Poems*, says 'invisible love has been an undercurrent in my poems'. Is this true of 'The Hug' in your opinion?

2. Reading a poem in the street sets everything in motion. List the things that happen as a result of that first action.

3. How would you describe the atmosphere on the street? Which details best capture the atmosphere in your opinion?

4. How would you describe the relationship between the speaker and her partner? Why is the speaker surprised?

5. Why is the detail 'He looks homeless because of how/ he needs' important?

6. Do you think the speaker describes the hug between herself and the stranger in the street well? Give reasons for your answer.

7. What do you think the speaker means by 'a masterpiece of connection'?

8. How do you interpret the poem's closing section?

9. How would you describe the personality of the speaker in 'The Hug'?

10. Do you like what is being described here? Would you like it to happen to you? Do you think it happens often? Give reasons for your answer.

11. This poem tells a story. Say why, in your opinion, it is not only a story but a poem.

Critical Commentary

The title suggests something warm and caring and loving. But the situation is a little unusual: an impulsive hug in the street. The speaker here is a poet and the hug is prompted by a poet and a poem – the woman reading a poem on the street. A small group of people have gathered to listened to the poem and the speaker is clearly struck by the fact that the poem 'is being read and listened to out here/ in the open'. It seems that time has stood still. The speaker mentions how 'no one is entering or leaving the houses'.

The moment described in the first stanza is both ordinary and special and has an effect on the speaker. Something happens unexpectedly: 'Suddenly a hug comes over me and I'm/ giving it to you'. It is a happy, intense moment and the speaker uses a simile of a shooting star to explain how she feels. There is this need within her to unload and to share her feeling of happiness.

There in the street the speaker hugs her partner and such is the effect of this that a homeless person asks for a hug. She says that 'we know he hasn't/ come out of nowhere'; this could suggest that the speaker is recognising the power of poetry. It made her give a hug to the person beside her; it also brought this person towards her for a hug.

Her partner has been hugged and he nods indicating that he is happy for this stranger to feel the warmth and generosity of a hug. The speaker is surprised – she thinks her hugs should only be for the one whom she loves and yet she goes to this other man, this stranger and gives him a hug.

The description of this hug, in stanzas three and four, is a description of something big and generous. Few people would choose to give a homeless person a hug but the speaker, though she questions and wonders at first, gives the hug her all. The details here allow us to see it and feel it clearly ['He's got an overcoat on/ so thick' . . . .'my hands not/ meeting behind his back . . . '] but there is also a whole other idea introduced into the poem at this point. When the speaker says 'we could be eternal' she is recognising that this moment is so special that it is somehow outside time, that it is part of eternity. And at line thirty-six the words we come across the shortest sentence in the poem: 'This hug.' The title is 'The Hug' and now we have 'This hug.'

This hug between the homeless man and the speaker is at the heart of the poem. It is an encounter that becomes a brief but meaningful moment. It is true and tender. The man is returning the hug and the speaker realises that this brief moment is such that everything else just doesn't seem to figure for that moment:

> we stop having arms and I don't know if
> my lover has walked away or what, or
> if the woman is still reading the poem, or the houses–
> what about them? – the houses

Her lover, the woman reading the poem, the houses for a very short time do not exist. All that exists is this current of feeling and connection between the huggers. That the houses are mentioned twice at this point is an interesting detail. Perhaps the speaker is reminding us that the homeless person in her arms has no house or home to go to anyway. But he has this hug to warm him.

The experience has clearly been important to the speaker. She herself has written a poem about it. In the poem's opening lines there was a sense of the speaker and her lover as 'we' and 'us'. In the closing lines she speaks in an 'I' voice. She will walk away, she will rejoin her lover but this unusual encounter in the street, all brought on by the reading of a poem, focuses on herself, an individual who has created what she calls 'a masterpiece of connection.'

Kerry Hardie (b.1951)

Kerry Hardie was born in Singapore in 1951. She grew up in County Down, studied English at York and after university worked for BBC radio in Belfast and Derry. Working in the north of Ireland during the Troubles, she said that she 'became fascinated with people who found themselves in a hard place and how they reacted to this place.' She now lives in County Kilkenny. Hardie published her first collection, *A Furious Place*, in 1996. Her second collection, *Cry for the Hot Belly* appeared in 2000 and *The Shy Didn't Fall* in 2003. Her novel, *Hannie Bennet's Winter Marriage* was published in 2000 and a second novel, *The Bird Woman*, in 2006. She was ill for many years with ME and she has written about this with clear-sightedness and without self-pity. Winner of the 1996 Friends Provident National Poetry Competition, in 2005 she was awarded [with Sinead Morrissey] the Michael Hartnett Poetry Prize. Reviewing her work in The Irish Times, George Szirtes wrote that 'The whole of her poetry is like the closing of a firm hand on something small but vital, then the hand opens and lets the vital thing go.' And Olivia O'Leary praised her first novel as follows: 'Spare and vivid. I have rarely seen the countryside she writes of described so beautifully.' Her most recent collection is *Only This Room* [2009] and she published a *Selected Poems* in 2011.

Daniel's Duck

for Frances

I held out the shot mallard, she took it from me,
looped its neck-string over a drawer of the dresser.
The children were looking on, half-caught.
Then the kitchen life – warm, lit, glowing –
moved forward, taking in the dead bird,   5
and its coldness, its wildness, were leaching away.

The children were sitting to their dinners.
Us too – drinking tea, hardly noticing
the child's quiet slide from his chair,
his small absorbed body before the duck's body,   10
the duck changing – feral, live –
arrowing up out of black sloblands
with the gleam of a river
falling away below.
Then the duck – dead again – hanging from the drawer-knob,   15
the green head, brown neck running into the breast,
the intricate silvery-greyness of the back;
the wings, their white bars and blue flashes,
the feet, their snakey, orange scaliness, small claws,
    piteous webbing,
the yellow beak, blooded,   20
the whole like a weighted sack –
all that downward-dragginess of death.

He hovered, took a step forward, a step back,
something appeared in his face, some knowledge
of a place where he stood, the world stilled,   25
the lit streaks of sunrise running off red
into the high bowl of morning.

She watched him, moving to touch, his hand out:
What is it, Daniel, do you like the duck?
He turned as though caught in the act,   30
Saw the gentleness in her face and his body loosened.
I thought there was water on it –
he was finding the words, one by one,
holding them out, to see would they do us –
but there isn't.   35
He added this on, going small with relief
that his wing-drag of sounds was enough.

Glossary

1 mallard: a widespread and familiar duck in Ireland. The colourful male has a yellow bill, a green shiny head, purple-brown breast and white collar. In flight the mallard reveals a blue patch on inner wing. Found on wetlands, there are about 23,000 breeding pairs in Ireland.

2 dresser: a kitchen cupboard with shelves above for storing and displaying crockery

6 leaching: draining away [in Old English leccan means 'to water'; the use of the word here is particularly appropriate since the mallard duck is out of its element – the water has drained away]

11 feral: wild [in Latin fera means 'wild animal']

12 sloblands: mud-flats

17 intricate: complicated, detailed

19 piteous: deserving pity

19 webbing: a reference to the duck's feet – the membrane between the toes of the swimming duck

37 wing-drag: the image in this instance refers to Daniel's feelings and it echoes the word 'downward-dragginess' in line 22

Questions

1. How would you describe the scene in this poem? Is it an everyday, ordinary one or is it an unusual one? Give reasons for your answer? Who are the 'I' and 'she' of line 1?

2. Is it possible to say who shot the mallard? Is it important to know who shot it?

3. Comment of the contrast between 'warm, lit, glowing' [line 4] and 'coldness' and 'wildness' [line 6].

4. In the second stanza the duck comes back to life? How does this happen? Why? Which words best capture 'the duck changing' best, in your opinion?

5. What is the effect of the detailed description of the shot mallard in stanza three? What feelings are you left with as you read this stanza?

6. In stanza four the speaker focuses on Daniel's response to the dead duck. Which details here, in your opinion, reveal how Daniel feels about the duck. How would you describe Daniel's thoughts and feelings at this point in the poem?

7. Why do you think the speaker refers to 'the high bowl of morning' [line 27]? Why is it significant in this context?

8. The poem ends with the child moving to touch the duck. How does Daniel react to the question 'What is it, Daniel, do you like the duck?'

9. How do you interpret the closing lines of the poem?

10. Imagine Daniel years later remembering this incident? Would he view it in the same way as an adult as he did as a child?

Critical Commentary

The title is simple and straightforward and could suggest that the duck, in this instance, is a child's toy. The opening words, however, offer a picture that involves violence and death: 'I held out the shot mallard'. That the speaker is holding the dead bird gives the poem a direct, immediate feeling.

The setting is indoors, a kitchen where adults and children are gathered at dinnertime. This is a place that should not be associated with violence and death but the dead mallard hanging in the kitchen close to where the people are eating creates a different atmosphere. The speaker tells us that the children noticed this difference but not for long.

> The children were looking on, half-caught.
> Then the kitchen life – warm, lit, glowing –
> moved forward . . .

The mallard has been shot, is dead, but life goes on. The words 'kitchen life' and 'dead bird' bring together these two separate worlds but the first stanza with its matter-of-fact details and the idea of the presence of the dead bird no longer making an impact –

. . . its coldness, its wildness, were leaching away . . .

suggest that the speaker accepts the situation, is not disturbed by it.
In the second stanza, however, the focus shifts to one of the children. This is Daniel and he is clearly fascinated and drawn to the dead bird hanging from the drawer on the dresser. The poet speaks of his 'quiet slide from his chair' and 'his small absorbed body' – details that highlight the boy's fascination with the duck. The key idea in this stanza is that of 'the duck changing'. The dead bird is brought back to life in the speaker's imagination. The change is from death to life. The duck is alive once more and the effect is that of being suddenly up and away, of being airborne:

> feral, live –
> arrowing up out of black sloblands
> with the gleam of a river
> falling away below.

The enclosed, cosy world of the kitchen is replaced by the expanse of sloblands, sky and a river in the distance. The duck, it would seem, has escaped, is free and flying and this is how Daniel imagines it. It is the speaker's description but it can also be read as a description of Daniel's imagination at work. He is standing before the dead bird but the poem suggests that the boy imagines the bird flying through the sky.

The third stanza brings us back to earth. Stanza three begins with a detailed physical description of the bird. The words 'dead again' highlights the difference between the flight of fancy and the reality. The duck has been shot but its magnificence is remembered in the beautiful colours:

> the green head, brown neck running into the breast,
> the intricate silvery-greyness of the back;
> the wings, their white bars and blue flashes,
> the feet, their snakey, orange scaliness, small claws,
> piteous webbing,
> the yellow beak, blooded

This cataloguing of the bird's features, from top to tail, – the head, the back, the wings, the feet, the beak – is effective. These lines ask us to dwell carefully on the lifeless duck.

The poem's title, containing the boy's name and duck, captures the central idea in the poem which is the effect of the dead duck on the young boy. It is Daniel's Duck and the final two stanzas focus on how Daniel reacts. He is obviously deeply struck by the presence of the dead mallard:

> He hovered, took a step forward, a step back.
> He responds physically but the speaker, closely observing the boy, realises that Daniel is also discovering, learning:
> something appeared in his face, some knowledge
> of a place where he stood

The death of an animal is sometimes a child's first experience of death and it brings sorrow. Daniel has to take on board the sad reality of the death of this beautiful mallard; it's a difficult lesson to learn and the poet uses an image to convey the powerful effect that this experience is having on him:

> the world stilled,
> the lit streaks of sunrise running off red
> into the high bowl of morning.

The pictures painted here suggest beginning and promise – 'sunrise' and 'the bowl of morning' – and, of course, the dead duck will never experience these ever again. It is as if the speaker is imagining Daniel thinking and understanding such thoughts even though he might not at this stage express them in this way.

In the final stanza the 'she' of line one plays an important part. The speaker observes very carefully the woman and child and how they interact. The woman, in this instance, is possibly Daniel's mother and the italicised lines records their spoken exchange.

The little boy having stepped forward and stepped back now wants to touch the duck. The woman is sensitive to the boy's situation and speaks gently. The boy relaxes, he 'saw the gentleness in her face and his body loosened' and when he speaks it is to convey a sensation of the duck having water on it. The duck lived in water, it is now dead but Daniel's thinking 'there was water on it-' suggests a mallard duck in its habitat.

The final lines in the poem are weighed down with sorrow. The reality is that Daniel was wrong about the water and he realises this: 'but there isn't' and this brings relief. Daniel sounds sad and he has no more to say.

•

This is a poem without end-rhyme. Hardie does use slant rhyme as in

> something appeared in his face, some knowledge
> of a place where he stood, the world stilled . . .

and a music is also created in the sounds and pauses and different line lengths. The poetry is also in the images, repetitions and the intense, concentrated feeling.

Brendan Kennelly (b.1936)

Brendan Kennelly was born on 17 April 1936 in Ballylongford, County Kerry, the third of eight children. At two he was sent to an aunt in Sligo, where he spent eighteen months: 'an experience like that leaves you feeling a bit of an outsider, with an innate sympathy for outsiders'. He won a scholarship to Trinity College, worked for the ESB for a while and later studied at the University of Leeds. He was appointed Professor of Modern English Literature at Trinity College in 1973. A prolific writer, his first collection (with Rudi Holzapfel) was *Cast A Cold Eye* in 1959 and since then he has published over twenty books of poetry, including *Cromwell* (1983), *The Book of Judas* 1991) *Poetry My Arse* (1995) and *The Man Made of Rain* (1998) which was written after he had major heart surgery, a quadruple bypass, in October 1996. He has also written versions of classical plays, including *Antigone, Medea, Blood Wedding* and two novels. The Oxford Companion to Irish Literature says that 'Throughout his work there is an impulse to let humanity speak of its disgrace as well as its loves, making his work a form of liberation'.

Night Drive

I

The rain hammered as we drove
Along the road to Limerick
'Jesus what a night' Alan breathed
And—'I wonder how he is, the last account
Was poor.'   5
I couldn't speak.

The windscreen fumed and blurred, the rain's spit
Lashing the glass. Once or twice
The wind's fist seemed to lift the car
And pitch it hard against the ditch.   10
Alan straightened out in time,
Silent. Glimpses of the Shannon—
A boiling madhouse roaring for its life
Or any life too near its gaping maw,
White shreds flaring in the waste   15
Of insane murderous black;
Trees bending in grotesque humility,
Branches scattered on the road, smashed
Beneath the wheels.
Then, ghastly under headlights,   20
Frogs bellied everywhere, driven
From the swampy fields and meadows,
Bewildered refugees, gorged with terror.
We killed them because we had to,
Their fatness crunched and flattened in the dark.   25
'How is he now?' Alan whispered
To himself. Behind us,
Carnage of broken frogs.

II

His head
Sweated on the pillow of the white hospital bed.   30
He spoke a little, said
Outrageously, 'I think I'll make it.'
Another time, he'd rail against the weather,

(Such a night would make him eloquent)
But now, quiet, he gathered his fierce will   35
To live.

III

Coming home
Alan saw the frogs.
'Look at them, they're everywhere,
Dozens of the bastards dead.'   40

Minutes later—-
'I think he might pull through now.'
Alan, thoughtful at the wheel, was picking out
The homeroad in the flailing rain
Nighthedges closed on either side.   45
In the suffocating darkness
I heard the heavy breathing
Of my father's pain.

Glossary

14 *maw:* stomach; Kennelly sees the raging Shannon as hungry and eager to draw 'any life' into it

17 *grotesque:* extravagant, distorted

28 *carnage:* slaughter

33 *rail:* use abusive language

34 *eloquent:* fluent, forceful use of language

44 *flailing:* beating, striking

Questions

1. In section I very little is said. Why? How would you describe the atmosphere in the car?

2. Do you think that Alan and the speaker respond differently to the father's illness?

3. Which words best capture the wild, stormy, threatening night? What does the weather contribute to the journey? Do you think that there might be a link between how the men in the car are feeling and the weather conditions outside?

4. How would you describe the mood in the different sections, I, II, III?

5. The poem describes the journey to the father's hospital bed, the hospital itself and the return journey. Do you think the poem offers a realistic account of how people respond to illness and pain?

6. Why do you think Kennelly included the description of the frogs?

7. How would you describe the poet's father as revealed to us in this poem? How would you describe the relationship between the poet and his father?

8. Would you say that Alan was a caring and sensitive man? Why did he drive over the frogs? What was his attitude towards them?

Critical Commentary

Here we have a narrative poem in free verse and the story told is straightforward. Two sons visit their ill father in hospital. The journey there is made on a very bad night weather-wise; their father is dying; they return home. The poem is made up of description of weather and place,' but Kennelly also includes the voices of his brother and father. He himself 'couldn't speak'.

Part I focuses on the difficulty of the journey west to visit their father. The wind, rain, the raging Shannon are all atmospherically captured here. The 'rain hammered', 'The windscreen fumed and blurred, the rain's spit/ Lashing the glass'. The sounds effectively convey the vicious night drive. But the journey is not only memorable for the bad weather, which could be read as an image of the troubled emotions the two sons are feeling within. Kennelly also includes the death of the frogs. The two brothers are very concerned about their father: 'I wonder how he is' and 'How is he now?' asks Alan, but the killing of the frogs is spoken of matter-of-factly:

> We killed them because we had to

Part II tells of the hospital visit and Kennelly indicates how ill his father really is when he says of him:

> He spoke a little, said
> Outrageously, 'I think I'll make it.'

The weather does not concern his father; his energies are directed towards what the poet calls his father's 'fierce will/ To live.

Part III presents us with two different views. Alan, it would seem, has taken his father's word – 'I think I'll make it' – at face value, whereas the speaker sees the road ahead as dark, unsettled, suffocating and somehow an image for his father's final journey:

> Nighthedges closed on either side.
> In the suffocating darkness
> I heard the heavy breathing
> Of my father's pain.

'Night Drive' is a poem that communicates immediately. It may seem simple, but the complicated, emotional heart of the poem is never made to seem easy. Sometimes words are inadequate; they do not do our feelings justice. In Kennelly's poem very little is said by the three men, but a great deal is felt and the feelings of the narrator are somehow explained by the descriptions of nature which make up most of the poem.

Michael Longley (b.1939)

Michael Longley, one of twin boys, was born in the Balmoral/Malone suburb of Belfast on 27 July 1939. Though part of a city, the houses on his road were surrounded by fields and, in an interview with Dermot Healy, Longley described the surrounding open countryside:

'. . . plenty of fields around the houses – playing fields, a field where a riding school trotted horses, a golf course, the remnants of ancient hedges, crab-apple trees like huge cradles, enough space in which to create your own wilderness. And a couple of miles away there was Barnett's Park, which sloped down to the Lagan and the towpath – and, a bit further west, the Minnowburn with its lanky, elegant beech trees; and then up a hilly road to the Giant's Ring, a dolmen set perfectly in a vast, circular grassy arena. I learned to love the contryside in South Belfast.'

His early background was non-literary for the most part, and Longley tells of the 'consternation and embarrassment at home' when in his early teens he chose Yeats's Collected Poems as a school prize. He was educated at the Royal Belfast Academical Institution and Trinity College, Dublin, where he studied classics.

Longley, speaking, in 1989, said of his schooling:
'At primary school (and later at grammar school) there was next to nothing on the curriculum to suggest that we were living on the island of Ireland and in the Province of Ulster: little or no Irish history except when it impinged on the grand parade of English monarchs; little or

no Irish literature; no Irish art; no Irish music. When we sang in music classes we mouthed English songs. One inspector criticised our accents and forced us to sing 'Each with his boony lawss, A-dauncing on the grawss.' A great deal of our schoolboy mythology was concerned with Roman Catholics. Why did Taigs cross themselves? What dark practices lurked behind confession and Mass? Didn't the nuns kidnap little girls and imprison them behind the suspiciously high walls of the big convent at the top of Ormeau Road? When ignorance and superstition replace curiosity and information the result is fear.

In the late Fifties and early Sixties when I attended Trinity College Dublin the two parts of Ireland were studiously incurious about each other. And it was the time of the Ban. The Catholic Church decreed that it was a mortal sin for Catholics to enroll at Trinity. I did become friendly with two Catholics – one an American and the other from Rhodesia! Not exactly The Real Thing! I didn't get to know The Real Thing until I returned to Belfast to teach. Poetry brought together a number of us in a way that denied sect and class. It now seems to me quite extraordinary that I was twenty-three before I could count Northern Irish Catholics among my close friends. This was when my education as an Ulsterman really began. And at this time I also began to discover 'the prophets' – John Hewitt, Estyn Evans, Michael J. Murphy, Lloyd Praeger, Louis MacNeice.'

And in an interview with Dermot Healy, Longley adds:
'At school the South of Ireland might just as well have been Outer Mongolia. But in the early '50s when my father could afford a car again, we used to drive to Dublin or just as far as Dundalk to buy sweets, which were still rationed in the North. A special treat for my twin and me was a Knickerbocker Glory in the Palm Grove Ice Cream Parlour in O'Connell Street; and then we'd chew iced caramels all the way home to Belfast. As good a way as any to find out about somewhere else. Caravan holidays in Donegal followed. My first glimpses of the landscape knocked me for six. In some ways my poetry is a vain attempt to recapture that wakening. By the time I was sixteen or seventeen it seemed quite natural to think of Trinity College as a university where I might study (though my parents were bewildered by my choice of subject: Classics). I went there in 1958. At that time the major grammar schools in the North traditionally sent their classical scholars to Trinity; the Catholic Church's ban still operated; and Oxbridge rejects from the English public schools came to Trinity as the next best. It wasn't as Irish a university as it is today. No, but it was Irish in its own way, and life there opened out spontaneously into the life of the city. I felt at home as an Ulsterman living in Dublin. And I certainly felt closer to Dubliners than to Etonians and Harrovians baying across Front Square – though I got to like some of them. My sense of Ireland continues to develop as I discover more of it. It's as simple as that. Last summer I explored West Cork for the first time, and dipped into County Carlow. I hate the notion that there are degrees of Irishness. One of the ways of defeating it is to experience as much of the island as you can.'

Longley's parents came from Clapham Common and settled in Belfast in 1927. His father served in World War I (he won the Military Cross) and World War II. By profession he was a commercial traveller and before the war he travelled the whole of Ireland, though shortly after the First World War he spent several years mining for gold and tin in Nigeria. The Second World War began in September 1939 and Longley's father was posted to England, where he remained two years. After World War II, when his sales job was no more, he worked as a professional fundraiser for charities, a life of early partial retirement. Longley's father died in 1960 when Longley was twenty. In his poetry, Longley frequently writes about the father-son relationship, for example in 'Wounds', 'Last Requests' and 'Laertes'.

After Trinity, Michael Longley taught in schools in Dublin, London and Belfast. In 1970 he joined the Arts Council of Northern Ireland, where he became Combined Arts Director, and is now retired.He is married to the lecturer and critic Edna Longley and they have three children.

Since the 1970s the Longleys have been going to the Thallabawn area of County Mayo for summer holidays, where their friends Michael and Ethna Viney live. There they stay in a remote cottage and in Longley's words: 'You have to cross water twice to reach the place. It's south of Louisburgh and north of Killary Harbour – in the shadow of Mweelrea. I'm not going to be more specific than that. Further clues are in the poems.' Speaking of the importance of this place, he told Clive Wilmer in a 1991 interview: 'When I go to the West of Ireland, I don't go there to have colourful talks with the natives. I go there to look at birds and flowers and the beautiful countryside. I am to some extent a disappointed solitary, a failed hermit. Ultimately, though I would hate to be putting over any glib green message, I think that our relationship with the natural world and with the plants and animals is the major issue now.'

Longley published his first collection, *No Continuing City*, in 1969, when he was thirty. There followed *An Exploded View* (1973), *Man Lying on a Wall* (1976), *The Echo Gate* (1979), *Poems 1963 – 1983* (1985), *Gorse Fires* (1991), *The Ghost Orchid* (1995), *Selected Poems* (1998) and *The Weather in Japan* (2000), and *Snow Water* (2004)'. *A Collected Poems* was published in 2006. His most recent collection is *A Hundred Doors* [2011].

Badger

for Raymond Piper

I
Pushing the wedge of his body
Between cromlech and stone circle,
He excavates down mine shafts
And back into the depths of the hill.

His path straight and narrow   5
And not like the fox's zig-zags,
The arc of the hare who leaves
A silhouette on the sky line.

Night's silence around his shoulders,
His face lit by the moon, he   10
Manages the earth with his paws,
Returns underground to die.

II
An intestine taking in
patches of dog's-mercury,
brambles, the bluebell wood;   15
a heel revolving acorns;
a head with a price on it
brushing cuckoo-spit, goose-grass;
a name that parishes borrow.

III
For the digger, the earth-dog   20
It is a difficult delivery
Once the tongs take hold,

Vulnerable his pig's snout
That lifted cow-pats for beetles,
Hedgehogs for the soft meat,   25

His limbs dragging after them
so many stones turned over,
The trees they tilted.

Glossary

TITLE Badger: a nocturnal, solitary, quiet, inoffensive, hibernating animal; it digs for itself a burrow, which it defends fiercely against attack. The badger does not usually seek to attack, but, when driven to bay, its great muscular power and tough hide render it a formidable protagonist.

Dedication: 'for Raymond Piper'; Raymond Piper is a self-taught botanist and portrait painter and a close friend of Longley's. The poem 'Badger' was born out of a conversation with Piper. Longley says that there are animals in all his books and he sees them as 'spirits or custodial presences in my mind and on the page.' The badger, according to Longley, is one of the most beautiful animals that we share the island with.

2 cromlech: a Welsh word (*crom* meaning bent and *llech* meaning flat stone), cromlech is also known as dolmen – a structure of pre-historic age consisting of a large flat unhewn stone resting horizontally on three or more stones set upright

2 stone circle: monuments which consist essentially of a circle of stones enclosing an open area, or, possibly, a space in which there is a small burial mound or a stone-built grave. All the ancient Celts revered stone, trees and so on. They believed in the consciousness of all things and believed that stones, especially, had an indwelling spirit. Stone circles are found in almost every part of Ireland and are still viewed as sacred places.

14 dog's-mercury: a common woodland herbaceous plant *(Mercurialis perennis)*

19 a name that parishes borrow: places such as Brockhampton, Brockhurst.

22 tongs: implement, consisting of two limbs connected by a hinge, by means of which their lower ends are brought together, so as to grasp and take up objects. Used here to remove the badger from the earth

23 vulnerable: open to attack or injury

Questions

1. The poem offers three different pictures of the badger. First, the badger at one with nature; second, some different perceptions of the badger; third, the badger being hunted. Consider the structure of the poem and the different form of each section.

2. In Part I what qualities does Longley admire in the badger? How does he create a sense of mystery? Why is the badger contrasted with the fox and the hare? What is the effect of this?

3. Just as Elizabeth Bishop in her poem 'The Fish' refers to the fish as 'he', Michael Longley also uses 'he' when referring to the badger in Parts I and III. Why not in Part II?

4. How would you describe the style of writing in Part II? Look at 'intestine', 'heel', 'head'. Has the tone changed from Part I to Part II? Explain.

5. The final section describes the badger hunt. Which words bring this vividly before the reader? Is there an irony in 'difficult delivery'? Comment on how Longley uses contrast in Part III.

6. Which details in the poem's final section win our sympathy for the badger?

7. How would you describe the overall effect of the poem?

Critical Commentary

Longley calls his poem 'Badger', not 'The Badger' or 'A Badger' and by so doing suggests that the poem is about all badgers, their individual, unique characteristics.

The poem is divided into three sections, each with a different focus, and in each section Longley uses a different method for shaping the words on the page. Section I uses three four-lined stanzas; the second section is a single stanza of seven lines; and section III has three three-lined stanzas. Longley does not use end-rhyme; alliteration, repetition and vivid images give the language its power.

In section I each stanza is a self-contained sentence. 'Badger' begins dramatically. Longley observes the badger, a nocturnal animal,

> Pushing the wedge of his body
> Between cromlech and stone circle

and the present tense of 'Pushing' gives the moment immediacy. The word 'pushing' with its stress on the first syllable, followed by the short, unstressed syllable, captures in its sound the act it describes. The 'cromlech' and 'stone circle' tell us that this is no ordinary landscape. The badger is pushing and digging 'Between cromlech and stone circle' and therefore there is the suggestion that the badger is associated with ancient and sacred places of ritual.

There is something mysterious in the badger's movements:

> He excavates down mine shafts
> And back into the depths of the hill.

He only comes out at night, spending his days in darkness; 'back into the depths of the hill' suggests an underworld of his own.

Stanza two compares the badger's movements to those of the fox and the hare, and Longley admires the badger's movements most:

> His path straight and narrow
> And not like the fox's zig-zags,
> The arc of the hare who leaves
> A silhouette on the sky line.

The cliché 'straight and narrow' implies an ordered, predictable way of life but Longley uses it here to highlight the superior movement of the badger who is direct and cautious compared to the devious, angled movement of the fox or the lightning speed of a hare on the horizon.

The badger achieves an almost human quality. Longley refers to him as 'he' and the image of excavating 'down mine shafts' and moving in a 'straight and narrow path' are also human terms.

This descriptive section ends with a moonlit detail and a sympathetic awareness of how the badger dies:

> Night's silence around his shoulders,
> His face lit by the moon, he
> Manages the earth with his paws,
> Returns underground to die.

This first section describes the badger pushing and digging its path and his returning to the earth to die. It works on its own as an observed piece but in the second and third sections Longley considers the badger from different perspectives and achieves a more complete picture.

In Section I the reader is aware that Longley likes and admires the badger's determined strength and purpose. The badger is alone, the badger 'Returns underground to die', evokes a sympathetic feeling towards the badger.

Section II is written in an impersonal way. Here the badger is no longer referred to as 'he'; its body is reduced to mere parts: an intestine, a heel, a head. And it is seen as an animal with a price on its head.

> An intestine taking in
> patches of dog's-mercury,
> brambles, the bluebell wood;
> a heel revolving acorns;
> a head with a price on it
> brushing cuckoo-spit, goose-grass;
> a name that parishes borrow.

In this one sentence a very different image of the badger emerges. What the badger eats and its ability to gather acorns are natural details. Then Longley thinks of the badger as endangered or threatened. This animal is valuable. There is a price on its head.

That same head is then described as it moves through the tall grasses 'brushing cuckoo-spit, goose-grass'. This is the head moving freely in its natural habitat, and there is an irony in the last line of this second section. It is ironic in that, though the badger is seen as an enemy and should be killed, its name has been incorporated into and celebrated in the name of the parishes.

Section III describes a badger hunt and, like section II, section III is one sentence long and its unstoppable movement describes the cruel way in which the badger is hauled from the earth. The badger is hounded and, instead of digging or excavating 'down mine shafts' as he was doing in stanza one, here the badger is being dug out of his burrow:

> For the digger, the earth-dog
> It is a difficult delivery
> Once the tongs take hold

There is a cruel irony in Longley's use of 'delivery'. This is not a birth but a death. The badger is being delivered into captivity. And against this ferociously cruel activity the closing lines of the poem remember the quiet delicate movements of the badger as it hunted for food:

> Vulnerable his pig's snout
> That lifted cow-pats for beetles,
> Hedgehogs for the soft meat,
>
> His limbs dragging after them
> So many stones turned over,
> The trees they tilted.

Here the badger, as in section I, is referred to as he – 'his pig's snout', 'his limbs' – and lines 23 – 25 describe the perfectly natural habits of the badger, searching for beetles and the 'soft meat' of hedgehogs.

The badger is dragged from its burrow with tongs – 'dragging', 'turned', 'tilted' suggest violence and disorder, the badger's frantic efforts to escape. The poem began with the badger excavating down, a natural activity. Being dragged out of the ground is by contrast unnatural and cruel.

John Milton (1608 – 1674)

John Milton was born on 9 December 1608 in Bread St, Cheapside, London, above his father's shop. He was the son of a scrivener [a drafter of documents; notary], composer and Puritan convert from a Catholic Oxfordshire family. He studied at Christ's College, Cambridge, where he began to write poems in Latin, Italian and English. His father's wealth allowed Milton financial independence and to devote his life to study and the writing of a great literary work. By twenty-one he had written 'Ode on the Morning of Christ's Nativity'; he wrote 'Lycidas' in 1637, when he was thirty. He travelled on the Continent in 1638 and met Galileo in Italy. For the next twenty years Milton wrote hardly any poetry in English, was very involved in politics and was imprisoned for his views. Charles I was beheaded in 1649 and that same year Milton was appointed Latin Secretary by Oliver Cromwell. Cromwell died in 1658 and the monarchy was restored by 1660. Milton was imprisoned for being anti-Royal but later pardoned. In 1642, when Milton was thirty-three, he had married Mary Powell, sixteen years his junior. She deserted him after six weeks and Milton produced four pamphlets advocating divorce on the grounds of incompatability. He began to lose his sight in the 1640s; his wife returned in 1645 and they had three daughters and a son who died in infancy. He was totally blind by 1651 and he dictated his work. In 1652 his first wife died and he married twenty-eight year old Katherine Woodcock in 1656. She died two years later, giving birth to a daughter who only lived a few months. In 1663 he married a third time. He died of gout on 8 November 1674 and is buried in the chancel of St Giles', Cripplegate. Milton's greatest work is *Paradise Lost* which was written over several years, beginning, it is thought, in 1658, finished in 1663 and published in 1667.

When I consider how my light is spent'

When I consider how my light is spent,
  E'er half my days, in this dark world and wide,
  And that one Talent which is death to hide,
  Lodg'd with me useless, though my Soul more bent
To serve therewith my Maker, and present   5
  My true account, least he returning chide,
  Doth God exact day-labour, light deny'd,
  I fondly ask: But patience to prevent
That murmur, soon replies, God doth not need
  Either man's work or his own gifts, who best   10
  Bear his milde yoak, they serve him best, his State
Is Kingly. Thousands at his bidding speed
  And post o'er Land and Ocean without rest:
  They also serve who only stand and waite.

Glossary

1 light: sight

1 spent: extinguished

3 one talent which is death to hide: on this instance, writing; a reference to the New Testament, Matthew 25, verses 14-30, which tells of the man who gave five talents to one servant, two to another and another one; 'to every man according to his separate ability'. Matthew says:'The man who had been given the five talents went and traded with the same, and made them other five talents. . . But he that had received one went and digged the earth, and hid his lord's money'. Later, when the master discovered what the servant did with the one talent he said 'Thou wicked and slothful servant'.

8 fondly: foolishly

8 prevent: stop

11 yoke: burden

11 state: splendour

13 post: travel quickly

This sonnet was written circa 1652 by which time Milton was entirely blind. He was forty-three in 1652 and when he says 'half my days' it would suggest that Milton did not think of the Biblical 'three score years and ten' as the natural life span but over eighty. Milton's father died at eighty-four.

Questions

1. At the heart of this sonnet is the question 'Doth God exact day-labour, light deny'd?' [Does God expect the same work from a blind man?]. How does Milton present the question? How would you describe the mood with which the poem begins?

2. How would you describe the relationship between the speaker and God?

3. What does the use of the word 'fondly' imply here?

4. The poem asks a question, it also answers it. How did Milton reach that answer? How would you describe the mood in the final line? Does his conclusion surprise you?

5. Do you think this a pessimistic or an optimistic poem? Give reasons for your answer.

6. Why is the word 'But' in line eight so important?

7. Trace the movement in the poem from complaint towards confidence. What do we learn about John Milton in this sonnet?

8. Why is the rhythm important here? How does the poem's movement mirror the poem's meaning?

Critical Commentary

Milton wrote this sonnet circa 1655, when he was in his forties, and it is one of Milton's first references in his poetry to his blindness which had begun to afflict him since 1644. By 1651 he was completely blind and this sonnet is structured in such a way that he asks a question of God and finds an answer.

The mood with which the poem begins is one of quiet disappointment. He believes in God, he is devoted to God, and he asks the very understandable question 'why did God deprive me of my sight?' In the opening lines the image presented of his life is a dark, negative, lonely one:

> When I consider how my light is spent,
>   E'er half my days in this dark world and wide

His eyesight is no more ['spent' means gone forever or lost] and the whole world is dark and empty. The words 'this dark world and wide' have a simple but powerful effect. Having been afflicted in this way the speaker thinks that, if his one God-given talent cannot be used, then his life will be a kind of death. To ignore one's talent is wrong, he considers it death to hide a talent and yet his talent is now useless.

His body, because of his blindness, is unable to serve his God in the way he had hoped, yet his soul is more determined than ever to worship his Maker:

> . . . that one Talent which is death to hide,
> Lodg'd with me useless, though my Soul more bent
> To serve therewith my Maker

Milton's disappointment and confusion give way to troubled and anxious thoughts of what God expects of him. Milton wants to do everything he should; his devotion to God is total and he does not want to be found lacking when God assesses how he has lived his life. Milton fears that God may chide or scold or rebuke him for not honouring Him sufficiently. Milton wants to

>   present
> My true account, least he returning chide

> and God is here portrayed as an authoritative figure, one who is almost feared.

Almost at the centre of the sonnet (line 7) is the central question:

> Doth God exact day-labour, light denied

which adds to the image of God as a demanding, exacting presence. The question is asked 'fondly' [which could mean 'foolishly' or 'tenderly' and both interpretations are valid] and the placing of the 'I fondly ask' at the end of the question suggests a humility on Milton's part:

Doth God exact day-labour, light deny'd,
I fondly ask

The sonnet turns on the word 'But' in line eight. The question has been asked and the answer is now given. Both question and answer originate in the speaker and, if a talent has been denied him, he has been given the gift of patience:

But patience to prevent
That murmur, soon replies, God doth not need
Either man's work or his own gifts, who best
Bear his milde yoak, they serve him best, his State
Is Kingly.

The one who serves God best, therefore, is the person who accepts his lot in life. God does not need man's efforts or man's gifts; in other words, God does not need man's talents which are in any case God-given, which would suggest that man is more in need of God than God in need of man, God being, in this instance, a majestic and distant presence.

Milton here speaks of a 'milde yoak' or easy burden, which would suggest that he has come to accept his blindness.
The sonnet's closing lines conjure up a picture of multitudes and busyness:

Thousands at his bidding speed
And post o're Land and Ocean without rest

This is a reference to the thousands of angels or messengers that do God's bidding ['angel' literally means 'messenger'; in Milton's Paradise Lost, Book IV, line 677-680 Milton says 'Millions of spiritual creatures walk the Earth/ Unseen, both when we wake and when we sleep;/ All these with ceaseless praise his works behold/ Both day and night.] It is an image of purposeful, never-ending activity. These messengers speed around the world serving their God. Milton is confined to a world of darkness and his movements are restricted, but there is a powerful and quiet dignity in the poem's concluding line:

They also serve who only stand and wait.

Milton will serve his God as he knows how. He cannot speed and post ('post' means to 'travel with haste') over land or across the seas as he believes God's angels do. He will serve God in his own way. He cannot do more and, in accepting God's purpose, he too is honouring and serving God.

Like line seven – 'Doth God exact day-labour, light deny'd' – the final line also consists almost entirely of strong, single-sounding or monosyllabic words. The two most memorable lines in the poem sum it up. One asks the question, the other answers it.

Paul Muldoon (b.1951)

Paul Muldoon was born on 20 June 1951 in Portadown, County Armagh, and grew up in Collegelands, where a small rural Roman Catholic community was surrounded by a predominantly Protestant parish of Loughgall where, in a village of the same name, the Orange Order was founded in 1795. At St Patrick's secondary school in Armagh, Muldoon, encouraged by his teachers, began to write poetry and in 1968 he met Michael Longley and Seamus Heaney at a poetry reading at Armagh Museum. Heaney was instrumental in publishing the seventeen-year-old Muldoon. 'Thrush' and 'Behold the Lamb' were Muldoon's first published poems. Muldoon studied at Queen's University, Belfast, from 1969-1973 and his first collection, *New Weather*, was published the year he graduated. He worked as a radio producer with the BBC in Belfast, resigned in 1985, lived in Dingle for nine months and, after a year teaching at Cambridge and the University of East Anglia, moved to the United States. He taught at Columbia, Berkeley, and the University of Massachusetts and in 1990 moved to Princeton, where he directs the Creative Writing Programme. His collections include *Mules* (1977), *Why Brownlee Left* ((1980), *Quoof* (1983), *Selected Poems* (1986), *Meeting the British* (1987), *Hay* (1998), *Poems 1968-1998* (2001), *Moy Sand and Gravel* [2002] which won the Pulitzer Prize, *Horse Latitudes* [2006] and *Maggot* [2010].

Anseo

When the Master was calling the roll
At the primary school in Collegelands,
You were meant to call back *Anseo*
And raise your hand
As your name occurred.   5
Anseo, meaning here, here and now,
All present and correct,
Was the first word of Irish I spoke.
The last name on the ledger
Belonged to Joseph Mary Plunkett Ward   10
And was followed, as often as not,
By silence, knowing looks,
A nod and a wink, the Master's droll
'And where's our little Ward-of-court?'

I remember the first time he came back   15
The Master had sent him out
Along the hedges
To weigh up for himself and cut
A stick with which he would be beaten.
After a while, nothing was spoken;   20
He would arrive as a matter of course
With an ash-plant, a salley-rod.
Or, finally, the hazel-wand
He had whittled down to a whip-lash,
Its twist of red and yellow lacquers   25
Sanded and polished,
And altogether so delicately wrought
That he had engraved his initials on it.

I last met Joseph Mary Plunkett Ward
In a pub just over the Irish border.   30
He was living in the open,
In a secret camp
On the other side of the mountain.
He was fighting for Ireland,
Making things happen.   35

And he told me, Joe Ward,
Of how he had risen through the ranks
To Quartermaster, Commandant:
How every morning at parade
His volunteers would call back *Anseo*   40
And raise their hands
As their names occurred.

Glossary

10 Joseph Mary Plunkett: the name of one of the leaders of the Easter 1916 Rising. Joseph Mary Plunkett (1887-1916) was one of the seven signatories to the Proclamation of the Irish Republic.
13 droll: odd, amusing
14 Ward-of-court: a pun on ward-of-court, a minor or insane person who is under the protection of the court
25 lacquers: protective resin coating
32 camp: an Irish Republican Army camp

Questions

1. Describe, in your own words, Joseph Mary Plunkett Ward's schooldays. Why is the word 'Anseo' ironic in this instance.

2. How would you describe the relationship between the Master and Joseph Mary Plunkett Ward? In stanza three how would you describe the relationship between Joe Ward and the volunteers?

3. In stanza two what do we learn of Joseph Mary Plunkett Ward? Why does he, in your opinion, engrave his initials on a stick with which he is about to be beaten?

4. Is this a personal or a political poem or both?

5. How would you describe Muldoon's use of language here? Give examples from the text.

6. Write a note on the similarities and differences between the two 'anseos'.

7. How does Paul Muldoon feel about Joe Ward's life as a grown-up? Is it possible to say?

Critical Commentary

On the page this poem has a very formal look; it is in effect three sonnets, each stanza has fourteen lines even if it doesn't have a regular end-rhyme or the even line length of the iambic pentameter. This formality is appropriate in a poem that explores rigid discipline and order.

The poem begins with a memory of the past. The scene is the speaker's class room in primary school and the atmosphere is one of regularity and control. The pupils know exactly how to behave, how to raise their hand and to speak in turn. The words 'All present and correct' could be said to sum up the scene except that things were not always 'present and correct': Ward was frequently absent. The speaker recalls how 'anseo' was the first word of Irish he spoke and how the word was associated with order, discipline, control.

The Master's powerful presence is conveyed in his droll

> 'And where's our little Ward-of-court?'

The speaker is one of a group where everyone is expected to know his place. Ward is immediately established as the outsider, the one who does not obey the school rules. He plays truant and to deviate in this way deserves punishment.

In stanza two Muldoon remembers how Ward, when he did return to school after his first truancy, was sent out to supply his own instrument of punishment. This became such a habit that on other occasions when Ward would skip school he would return prepared. Stanza one describes the predictable but stanza two contains an interesting detail: when Ward knew he was going to be punished he would not only supply the stick but he would fashion it with delicacy and care. There was an artistry in the way he created the instrument of violence:

> He would arrive as a matter of course
> With an ash-plant, a salley-rod.
> Or, finally, the hazel-wand
> He had whittled down to a whip-lash,
> Its twist of red and yellow lacquers
> Sanded and polished,
> And altogether so delicately wrought
> That he had engraved his initials on it.

Words such as 'whittled', 'Sanded', 'polished', 'delicately wrought', 'engraved' suggest care and attention and a sense of ceremony. And the carving of his initials on the stick is an ironic touch. Though he is being beaten by a teacher, the fact that he has named himself on the stick somehow suggests that Ward is in control of the situation, not the Master.

The final stanza moves to the more recent past. Whereas he was once the outsider, the truant, Ward is now grown up and he belongs by choice to another group, a group even more disciplined than those in a classroom. The irony in the closing lines are obvious but the speaker recounts the situation without comment. Joseph Mary Plunkett Ward has become the more manageable, the less comical, the less political Joe Ward but Ward's life now is totally political and it is he who is in control. The teacher once called out the names and Ward was missing. Ward himself now calls the roll and the volunteers answer back 'Anseo' echoing the classroom procedure all those years ago.

Now Joe Ward is someone who is

> Making things happen.

He is fighting for Ireland, he is caught up in a cause and 'living in the open,/ In a secret camp'. When he was young he was victim yet even then he displayed an individuality and determination in the very way he fashioned the stick 'with which he would be beaten'. Now he is a leader of men.

Nowhere does the poet reveal how he himself feels about Joe Ward the boy or the man. He presents the facts of the story and yet he conveys how complex the world of the North of Ireland is. Muldoon himself says that 'Anseo' is about a very complex society indeed'.

•

This poem had been described as a poem about conditioning and tells of how behaviour can condition a person in a rather chilling way. Speaking about 'Anseo', Muldoon says that if the poem works, 'it works because everything in it is absolutely dead-on, the details in it are really accurate. It's fiction, of course.'

Clair Wills in her book *Reading Paul Muldoon* says of 'Anseo': Joseph Mary Plunkett Ward is the school rebel, and persistent truant. he is rarely present for the calling of the roll. . . . His punishment is to be beaten by the master, with a stick he has found himself in the hedges . . . . Not only does he make his own means of punishment but he also makes it his own - he engraves his initials on the stick used to beat him which is then, literally, 'a rod for his own back'. Eventually Ward takes a place within the hierarchy of the IRA which is equivalent to that of the Master of the school'.

'A great many things are going on in this poem' says Clair Wills, ' — there is firstly the similarity between the disciplinary institutions of school and revolutionary army, the use of Irish to enforce a sense of belonging, the linking of the Irish language, nationalism and education. . . . The poem sets up a contrast between the writer and the activist revolutionary; the latter is "making things happen" as opposed to the passive occupations of reading and writing. But in reality poet and revolutionary share a great deal, for ward is also an artist. He creates "delicately wrought" art out of his method of punishment, but perhaps more telling is his name. Joseph Mary Plunkett was a poet, friend of Patrick Pearse, and one of the signatories to the 1916 Declaration of Independence, who was executed after the Easter Rising. Ward then is named after a poet-revolutionary, but even his surname reveals his writerly bent . . . . ward means "son of the court" (Mhac an Bhaird). So Joseph Mary Plunkett Ward is a poet/revolutionary twice over, and the contrast between him and the Muldoon figure is in fact a comparison.'

Julie O'Callaghan (b.1954)

Chicago born, Julie O'Callaghan has lived in Dublin since 1974 and now lives in Naas. As a child she was asked by a teacher to write a poem for homework. 'I went home and wrote a poem in the shape of a tree – the branches were the various lines of the poem. Why I did that I have no idea – maybe it was because I was missing the elm tree that the city of Chicago had chopped down outside our house and it seemed like a good way to bring it back.' She also drew the outline of her hand and wrote within its borders a self-portrait. These exercises inspired her to become a writer. Julie O'Callaghan works part-time in the Library at Trinity College and has published several collections including *Edible Anecdotes* [1983], *What's What* [1991], *No Can Do* [2000], *Tell Me This is Normal* [2008] and for younger readers, *Taking My Pen For A Walk* (1988), *Two Barks* (1998), *The Book of Whispers* [2006] and *Tell Me This Is Normal – New and Selected Poems* [2008]. O'Callaghan says: 'The poet takes language, condenses it, charges it with energy, gives it a bit of oomph – and there's the poem! O'Callaghan was elected to Aosdána in 2003.

Problems

Take weeds for example.
Like how they will overrun
your garden and your life
if you don't obliterate them.
But forget about weeds   5
-- what about leaves?
Snails use them as handy
bridges to your flowers
and hordes of thuggish slugs
will invade – ever thought about that?   10
We won't even go into
how leaves block up the gutters.
I sure hope you aren't neglecting
Any puddles of water in your bathtub
-- discoloration will set in.   15
There is the wasp problem,
the storms problem, the grass
growing-between-the-bricks-in-the-driveway problem.
Then there's the remembering to
lock-all-the-windows problem.   20
Hey, knuckleheads!
I guess you just don't appreciate
How many problems there are.

Glossary

4 obliterate: destroy completely
9 hordes: large groups
9 thuggish: violent and aggressive and hostile
15 discoloration: fading, duller colouring
21 knucklehead: a stupid person

Questions

1. Problems, problems, problems. Hassle, hassle, hassle. Give some of your own examples.

2. Do the problems listed here [weeds; leaves (leading to slugs and blocked gutters); wasps; storms; locking windows (or else you may be burgled)] match your own ideas of problems? Why? Why not?

3. How would you describe the speaker in the poem? Anxious? Neurotic? Exaggerating?

4. How would you describe the tone of voice in the poem? Look at the question marks, the use of italics, and the exclamation mark.

5. Do you think that it is important to listen to the speaker in 'Problems'? Give reasons for your answer.

6. The author is American? Which phrases suggest an American voice?

7. Is this a funny or a serious poem?

8. Why does the speaker say 'Hey, knuckleheads!'

9. Listen to how the poem's movement and music. Is it more like jazz than a symphony? Explain your answer.

10. Suggest some reasons why this poem was prescribed for Leaving Certificate. What advice would you give the poet?

Critical Commentary

The voice in 'Problems' is quirky and lively and a little stressed. It's a voice that is obsessed with problems of a domestic nature. If people were asked to draw up a list of problems they might not include any or all of the items mentioned here. Everyone has his/her own outlook on life and not everyone would view weeds or leaves as a problem.

Such is this speaker's view of things that leaves in themselves are a problem – 'they will overrun/ your garden' – but the speaker is so obsessed with problems of all kinds that she sees leaves as things that lead to other problems. Snails use them to get to flowers and they can also block gutters and drains.

Puddles of water in the bathtub is an indoors problem and then she jumps to the problem with wasps and grass and having to remember to lock the windows.

The tone is very immediate throughout and she is very anxious to get the reader onside in terms of recognising these problems and agreeing with her. The opening line is direct and it sounds as if she is already in full flight. No introduction. She jumps straight into her first example. Then abandons the topic when she suddenly seems to think of another one, and another one.

To these problems, problems, problems, the speaker offers no solutions.

Mary Oliver (b.1935)

Mary Oliver was born in Cleveland, Ohio, on 10 September 1935 and was educated at Ohio University and Vassar but did not finish her degree in either university. Winner of the Pulitzer Prize, the National Book Award, the Lannan Literary Award, in 1999 she received the New England Book Award for Literary Excellence. She has written over ten collections of poems and has lived in Provincetown on Cape Cod since 1964. She rarely gives interviews and has lived a private life with Molly Malone Cook her life partner, who died in 2005 and to whom she has dedicated many of her books. Stanley Kunitz says that 'Mary Oliver's poetry is fine and deep, it reads like a blessing.' And Oliver herself says: 'I see something and look at it and look at it. I see myself going closer and closer just to see it better, as though to see its meaning out of its physical form. And then, I take something emblematic from it and then it transcends the actual.'

The Sun

Have you ever seen
anything
in your life
more wonderful

than the way the sun,   5
every evening,
relaxed and easy,
floats toward the horizon

and into the clouds or the hills,
or the rumpled sea,   10
and is gone—
and how it slides again

out of the blackness,
every morning,
on the other side of the world,   15
like a red flower

streaming upward on its heavenly oils,
say, on a morning in early summer,
at its perfect imperial distance—
and have you ever felt for anything   20

such wild love—
do you think there is anywhere, in any language,
a word billowing enough
for the pleasure

that fills you,   25
as the sun
reaches out,
as it warms you

as you stand there,
empty-handed—   30
or have you too
turned from this world—

or have you too
gone crazy
for power,   35
for things?

Glossary

10 rumpled: untidy, ruffled
19 imperial: majestic, magnificent, commanding
23 billowing: expansive, full

Questions

1. The poem in a single sentence asks a question. How would you describe the movement of the poem as you read down through its thirty-six lines?

2. Do you believe the speaker when she says that there is nothing more wonderful than the sun? Are you convinced? Why?

3. Choose three striking pictures from this poem and draw them. What does the experience reveal?

4. The poem speaks directly to 'you'? What does the speaker hope for everyone? What does she think of 'power', of 'things'. What, in your opinion, is she referring to here?

5. Why, according to this poem, are sunrises and sunsets important? What effect do sunrises and sunsets have on us?

6. The poem speaks of 'wild love' and 'pleasure'. Comment of the significance of this.

7. How would you describe the speaker's tone of voice in lines 31-36.

8. The speaker says that words are inadequate when it comes to praising or honouring the sun and the way it makes us feel. Do you think Mary Oliver has conveyed well the power, beauty, mystery of the sun? Give reasons for your answer.

Critical Commentary

'The sun rises in spite of everything' is a marvellous, heartening line from Derek Mahon's poem 'Everything Is Going To Be All Right' and Mary Oliver's poem is a hymn to the sun. It is also a reminder that the sun is a gift, it is beautiful and vital and free.
The voice here is very confident from the opening line:

> Have you ever seen
> anything
> in your life
> more wonderful . . . .

Clearly she thinks not. The sun, its daily coming and going, is the most wonderful thing in the world. Such is the speaker's confidence that there is no stopping her. The poem is thirty-six lines long but only one full-stop is used and that's the question mark used at the end of the final line.

The poem paints pictures of sunset and sunset:

> . . . . the sun
> every evening,
> relaxed and easy,
> floats towards the horizon
>
> and into the clouds or the hills,
> or the rumpled sea,
> and is gone –
> and how it slides again
>
> out of the blackness,
> every morning,
> on the other side of the world

and the details are visual and sensuous. The sun is personified – it's relaxed and easy – and 'clouds', 'hills', 'rumpled sea' offer a range of settings.

A simile such as 'like a red flower' captures both colour and shape and something beautiful and the idea of the sun 'streaming upwards on its heavenly oils' suggests smooth movement, an other-worldly event.

The poem begins with high praise for the sun and the second section [beginning line 20, 'and have you ever felt . . . .'] focuses on the effect the sun has on us, or at least the person being addressed in the poem. The use of 'you' throughout ['you' is used six times] concentrates and personalises the experience of reading the poem in a very direct and effective way. The reader is involved from the outset and the speaker's tone grows stronger with each 'you'.

The sun allows us to experience 'wild love' and 'pleasure' and such feelings, it would seem, are impossible to put into words:

> do you think there is anywhere, in any language,
> a word billowing enough
> for the pleasure
> that fills you

The poem paints a picture of you the reader standing before the sun and the 'you' is 'empty-handed'. This is an interesting choice of adjective. Imagine if the space were blank and you were invited to choose an adjective to insert in that very line, what would you choose? Mary Oliver, in using 'empty-handed' suggests that the sun is the ultimate giver of gifts; there is no need for us to own anything, to hold anything in our hands.

The relationship between you and the sun is unique, is special. The sun 'reaches out' and 'warms you' and everything is wonderful.

But the poem does not stop there. Another idea is introduced in the final six lines, a challenging idea, a wake-up call. The speaker believes in the power and the beauty of the sun but the speaker also believes that some people have become blind to the beauty of the natural world. Materialism and power have infected our lives, have made us crazy and if we go down that road we become disconnected from the great giver of life, the majestic, magnificent, 'imperial' sun.

The poem speaks a simple but memorable idea and the movement of the poem is well-handled. Short lines, the use of commas, the use of repetition ['you', 'and', 'for', 'or'] create a powerful persuasive poem. The 'blackness/ every morning' is made bright every day and the speaker's tone is filled with wonder, praise, appreciation, at the thought of the miracle that is the sun, and eventually frustration when she realises that some have turned from nature and become more interested in 'power'and 'things'.

Marge Piercy (b.1936)

Marge Piercy, poet, novelist, essayist, was born on 31 March 1936 in
Detroit. Her family background is Jewish and working-class. She began
writing in her teens and was educated at the University of Michigan and
Northwestern University. Her writing stems from her political commitment
which began with the anti-Vietnam and Women's Movements of the
1960s. She says 'I imagine that I speak for a constituency, living and
dead.' Of herself and her work, she says 'you have to know why, you
have to know who you are, you have to know what you're doing and why
you're doing it. You have to know what you believe in . . . . That's mostly
poetry.' She has been married three times and now lives on Cape Cod in
Massachusetts with her husband, writer Ira Wood, and four cats. They
rise at six a.m. and write in separate offices.

Will we work together?

You wake in the early gray
morning in bed alone and curse
me, that I am only
sometimes there. But when
I am with you, I light   5
up the corners, I am bright
as a fireplace roaring
with love, every bone in my back
and my fingers is singing
like a tea kettle on the boil.   10
My heart wags me, a big dog
with a bigger tail. I am
a new coin printed with
your face. My body wears
sore before I can express   15
on yours the smallest part
of what moves me. Words
shred and splinter.
I want to make with you
some bold new thing   20
to stand in the marketplace,
the statue of a goddess
laughing, armed and wearing
flowers and feathers. Like sheep
of whose hair is made   25
blankets and coats, I want
to force from this fierce sturdy
rampant love some useful thing.

Glossary

1 early gray: echoing Earl Grey, a type of tea?
14 wears sore: becomes sore
18 shred and splinter: fall apart and break up
20 bold: courageous, brave, daring
23 armed: carrying weapons
27 fierce: intense [and a play on Pierc[y]?
27 sturdy: powerful, strong
28 rampant: flourishing, spreading unchecked

Questions

1.What do you think the title means? Does work here mean what it usually means? How can you tell? Can work be interpreted in different ways?

2. Why do you think her lover 'in bed alone' curses her for not being there 'in the early grey morning'?

3. How does she feel about being cursed?

4. How does she set about making up to him?

5. Would you describe the speaker as a confident woman. Why?

6. List the different images [similes and metaphors] that she uses to describe herself. What do they tell us about her?

7. How would you describe the effect of 'I want [line 19] and I want [line 26]?

8. Comment on the words 'with you' at line 19.

Critical Commentary

The title poses a question. The speaker asks her lover if he and she will work together. This could refer to their day-job which is writing but it could also refer to their relationship – will they get on together, will their relationship work well?

The poem is an intimate, personal address. It is also both honest and confident. When the speaker describes how sometimes her lover wakes 'in bed alone' and curses because 'I am only/ sometimes there' it could mean that she is not at home or that she has risen before her lover or it could mean, perhaps, that she is beside him but is away in a world of her own. Writers live inside their heads some of the time and perhaps Marge Piercy is speaking of the creative process, how when the writer is thinking, imagining you are in another place.

The words 'But when / I am with you' turn the poem around and the cursing and the feeling of being alone are no more. From this point on in the poem everything is generous and positive and filled with longing. The speaker gives herself to her lover, body and mind and imagination.

The imagery, lines 4 to the end, is filled with light and movement:

> But when
> I am with you, I light
> up the corners

and the tone becomes more and more confident as simile and metaphor paint one colourful, vivid picture after another:

> I am bright
> as a fireplace roaring
> with love, every bone in my back
> and my fingers is singing
> like a tea kettle on the boil

The fireplace and the kettle belong in the home; they are domestic, familiar images [similes]. The tone is very upbeat. She describes the feeling within her when she is with her lover, the words 'bright' and 'singing' give the language energy.

The metaphors that follow also add to the speaker's intense expression of her love:

> My heart wags me, a big dog
> with a bigger tail. I am
> a new coin printed with
> your face.

The 'big dog' and 'new coin' are fresh, memorable, physical images. Heart and face suggest closeness.

In twenty-eight lines the speaker uses 'I' eight times and though she is open and direct she also admits that words can not truly express how she feels:

> My body wears
> sore before I can express
> on yours the smallest part
> of what moves me.

Language is inadequate, words 'shred and splinter' and can not what she is feeling deep inside.

The poem ends with a key idea:

> I want to make with you
> some bold new thing

Here she and he are together; she wants them to work together to create a statue of a goddess and the poem's final, long, flowing sentences [lines 19-28] is filled with images an of grandeur, beauty, strength – that of the 'goddess/ laughing, armed and wearing/ flowers and feathers'. And then there follows a very unusual image, especially for a love poem, that of sheep. The speaker wants her love to grow and grow and give warmth and comfort

> Like sheep
> of whose hair is made
> blankets and coats

The speaker ends with a description of her love as 'fierce sturdy/ rampant' and the final adjective, 'useful', suggests something unstoppable and practical.

The poem began in a low-key voice, a double bed and an absent lover but this poem gains more and more energy and ends on a high, celebratory, generous note. It explores a physical and creative relationship and the reference to dog, bird, ['feathers'], sheep gives it a strong animal quality; it is a love poem that celebrates both body and mind.

Penelope Shuttle (b.1947)

Penelope Shuttle was born in 1947 in Staines, Middlesex and has lived in Falmouth, Cornwall since 1970. She began publishing in her twenties and won the Greenwood Prize [1972] an Eric Gregory Award [1974] and the Cholmondeley Prize [2007]. She has also written drama, fiction, non-fiction and collaborated with her husband, the poet Peter Redgrove, on several works. When he died she wrote a series of poems mourning and celebrating him; these were published as *Redgrove's Wife* (2006). Shuttle says that 'In my poetry I give primacy to the breath. For me it is the way the poem breathes that gives it form.'And in an author statement she writes: 'Without writing (and reading) life would be a drifting chaos for me, a series of losses and forgettings. My sense of being would have no meaning, no inner or outer geography. With writing (and reading) active in my life, I can concentrate on the chaos, hold experience steady. I can explore, enjoy, mourn, comprehend within my own limits, and keep pushing them as far as I can. Language is a key that unlocks the gates of paradise and the gates of hell. It is bliss and danger. It transforms feeling and experience into poetry. Poetry then becomes the mirror where self and world find a place to begin, a journey to continue – through the vivid and living reflection of language.' The poem 'Jungian Cows' is from Shuttle's 1988 collection *Adventures With My Horse*, a collection that explores human sexual awareness.

Jungian Cows

In Switzerland, the people call their cows
Venus, Eve, Salome, or Fraulein Alberta,
beautiful names
to yodel across the pastures at Bollingen.

If the woman is busy with child or book,   5
the farmer wears his wife's skirts
to milk the most sensitive cows.

When the electric milking-machine arrives,
the stalled cows rebel and sulk
for the woman's impatient skilful fingers   10
on their blowzy rosy udders,
will not give their milk;

so the man who works the machine
dons cotton skirt, all floral delicate flounces
to hide his denim overalls and big muddy boots,   15
he fastens the cool soft folds carefully,
wraps his head in his sweetheart's sunday-best fringed scarf,
and walks smelling feminine and shy among the cows,

till the milk spurts, hot, slippery and steamy
into the churns,   20
Venus, Salome, Eve, and Fraulein Alberta,
lowing, half-asleep,
accepting the disguised man as an echo of the woman,
their breath smelling of green, of milk's sweet traditional climax.

Glossary

TITLE Jungian: relating to Carl Gustav Jung (1875-1961), Swiss psychiatrist, who invented the word 'complex' and introduced the concepts of 'introvert' and 'extrovert'. Jung developed the theory of the 'collective unconscious'

2 Venus, Eve, Salome: Names of some of the more famous women in myth and history: Venus - The Goddess of Beauty and Love; Eve – the first woman; Salome – the woman who danced for Herod and was rewarded with the head of John the Baptist [cf. Mark 6. 17-28; Matthew 14. 1-12]

2 Fraulein: 'Miss' in German

4 yodel: sing or shout using a rapidly changing voice from ordinary voice to falsetto [forced high voice]

4 Bollingen: a small village near Rapperswil, in the Canton of St. Gallen, Switzerland. It is located on the north bank of Lake Zurich. It is well known as the location of the country retreat, a small castle with several towers, which Carl Jung built in the village on the shore of the lake. For much of his life Jung spent several months a year living at Bollingen, and here he accomplished much of his writing, painting, and sculpture.

9 stalled: enclosed, confined

9 sulk: become bad-tempered

11 blowzy: fat, coarse

11 udders: the organs, hanging near the hind legs, containing the mammary gland of the female cow where milk is stored

14 dons: puts on, dresses in

14 floral: with a flower pattern

14 flounces: frills, hanging dceorative strips sewn on a skirt

19 spurts: gushes out suddenly in a small stream

20 churns: large milk cans

22 lowing: mooing

24 climax: an intense, exciting, thrilling moment; the high point

Questions

1. Do you believe what you are being told in this poem? Why? Why not?

2. The speaker paints an interesting and unusual picture of farm life. Which details create this interesting and unusual picture?

3. What kind of a relationship exists, according to the speaker, between women and cows?

4. Comment on the difference between milking by hand and electric milking-machines. How do the cows respond to both?

5. What differences are identified between men and women in the poem?

6. Women are thought to be more caring and sensitive than men. In stanza four the man who works the machine dresses up as a woman. What does that tell us about the man?

7. Comment on the phrase 'man as an echo of the woman'.

8. Can you suggest why the poem is called 'Jungian Cows'? Is it possible to say why Penelope Shuttle wrote this poem?

Critical Commentary

If this poem were called 'Cows' it would present us with different and straightforward expectations. Add 'Jungian' and the poem becomes more complicated, perhaps even off-putting. But the poem turns the familiar into something unusual, interesting and amusing.

Many people have pet names for their animals but when we read that

> In Switzerland, the people call their cows
> Venus, Eve, Salome, or Fraulein Alberta

The names themselves are striking and the tone suggests that every cow is called one of these four names. The poet then paints a curious picture of the Swiss yodelling these names 'across the pastures at Bollingen'. The sounds of sing-song voices calling out the names of some of the most famous women's names in myth and history is funny and surreal.

One of the main ideas in this poem is the strong and important bond between women and cows. We learn that cows can be so sensitive that they clearly prefer to be handled by women, so much so, that the men have developed ways and means of fooling the cows into thinking that they are women:

> If the woman is busy with child or book,
> the farmer wears his wife's skirt
> to milk the most sensitive cows.

The woman is portrayed here in a nurturing or caring role – she is a mother; the woman is also intelligent – she is a reader. Her farmer husband tries to become her in order to get the best milking result from his cows. Here the male is acknowledging special female skills and is prepared to abandon his "manhood" briefly by dressing us as a woman. Stanza three tells how modern developments and advancements add a new difficulty. The cows have rejected men; now they reject technology:

> When the electric milking-machine arrives,
> the stalled cows rebel and sulk

because they want to be milked by

> the woman's impatient skilful fingers
> on their blowzy tough rosy udders

Impatient and skilful are interesting details. The woman is practical and practised but the cows prefer her touch. The cows clearly see the machine as unacceptable and reject it. They 'will not give their milk'.

Earlier in the poem when the farmer's wife was too busy, her husband pretended to be her so that 'the most sensitive cows could be milked'. Stanza four tells of the more recent developments – the milking-machine.

Now it is a different man who dresses up as a woman. He borrows his sweetheart's clothes; he goes to some trouble; he

> dons cotton skirt, all floral delicate flounces
> to hide his denim overalls and big old muddy boots,
> he fastens the cool soft folds carefully,
> wraps his head in his sweetheart's Sunday-best fringed scarf,
> and walks smelling feminine and shy among the cows

Here the farm worker is willing to change his appearance and do what many men would not enjoy doing; it could be said, to use some jargon, that he is willing to explore his feminine side. The picture of a man flowing and feminine, walking down a milking parlour is absurd but the results are spectacular. We are told that the ruse works. The male "feminine" touch is such that

> till the milk spurts, hot, slippery and steamy
> into the churns

The cows have been duped. They are content; they are 'lowing, half-asleep'. They think that they are being attended to by a woman and they have even accepted the mechanical milking-machine. The closing lines of the poem spell out what has happened. The cows have accepted 'the disguised man as an echo of the woman' and the poem's final line brings together the journey that begins with cows eating green grass out of doors and that ends with the spurting, hot, slippery, steamy milk into the churns. The poem's final word is 'climax' and seeing that this is a poem with Jung in the title the use of climax here may hint at Jung's interest in the collective unconscious and sexuality.

Some poems are written in the first person; the word 'I' does not occur in this poem which suggests that it is not personal. It is, however, a poem of ideas and observation and imagination. We can not tell if all the details in the poem are true but that does not prevent us from enjoying it as an original and memorable and interesting poem.

Peter Sirr (b.1960)

Peter Sirr was born in Waterford in 1960 and studied at Trinity College and lived abroad in the Netherlands and Italy for a number of years. At twenty-two he won the Patrick Kavanagh Award. Poet, freelance writer, editor and translator, he now lives in Dublin with his wife, the poet Enda Wyley, and their daughter. 'I think of poetry as an adventure' says Sirr. 'There are lots of signs, signals, but no real maps, no sure paths. Poets live in a noisy cave ful of tempting sounds; sometimes they might reach out and grab, as onto a handrail, led by a melody, a phrase, a ghost of something . . . . All the poetry I like has adventure and curiosity at its centre and those qualities bring a lot of other things in their wake too: an interest in the possibilities of language, a freshness of perspective that comes out of really seeing things.'

His books include *Marginal Zones* [1984], *Talk, Talk* [1987], *Ways of Falling* [1991], *The Ledger of Fruitful Exchange* [1995], *Bring Everything* [2000]. *Nonetheless* [2004], *Selected Poems* [2004], *The Thing Is* [2009]. He is a member of Aosdána.

Madly Singing in the City

after Po Chü-i

And often, when I have finished a new poem,
I climb to the dark roof garden
And lean on a rail over an ocean of streets.
What news I have for the sleeping citizens
And these restless ones, still shouting their tune   5
In the small hours. Fumes rise from the chip-shop
and I am back at the counter, waiting my turn.
Cod, haddock, plaice, whiting.
The long queue moves closer;
men in white coats paint fish with batter,   10
chips leap in the drying tray.
There's a table reserved for salt and vinegar
where the hot package is unswaddled,
salted, drenched, wrapped again
and borne out into the darkness.   15
In darkness I lean out, the new words ready,
The spires attentive. St Werburgh's, St Patrick's, Nicholas
Of Myra. Nearby the Myra glass company
from where we carried the glass table-top.
In a second I will sing, it will be as if   20
a god has leaned with me, having strolled over
from either of the two cathedrals, or from the green
and godly domes of Iveagh Buildings.
Ever since I was banished from the mountains
I have lived here in the roar of the streets.   25
Each year more of it enters me, I am grown
Populous and tangled. The thousand ties of life
I thought I had escaped have multiplied.
I stand in the dark roof garden, my lungs swelling
with the new poem, my eyes filled with buildings   30
and people. I let them fill, then,
without saying a word, I go back down.

Glossary

after Po Chü-I : [Bo Juyi] an eight-century/ ninth-century Chinese poet [772-846 AD] of the Tang dynasty. He was born in Shaanxi (Shensi) province and became governor in 831. His lyric poems were so admired that his poems were collected, by imperial order, and engraved on stone tablets. In all, he wrote 3,000 poems, one of which is called 'Madly Singing in the Mountains'. The closing lines of the poem [in a translation by Arthur Waley] are as follows:

> Half my time I have lived among the hills.
> And often, when I have finished a new poem,
> Alone I climb the road to the Eastern Rock.
> I lean my body on to the banks of white Stone;
> I pull down with my hands a green cassis branch.
> My mad singing startles the valleys and hills;
> The apes and birds all come to peep.
> Fearing to become a laughing-stock to the world,
> I choose a place that is unfrequented by men

4 news: Perhaps echoing Ezra Pound saying that 'Literature is the news that stays news'.
13 unswaddled: unwrapped
17 St Werburgh's: Dubin church
17 St Patrick's: Dublin cathedral, thirteenth century
17/18 Nicholas of Myra: Dublin church
22 two cathedrals: St Patrick's and Christchurch
23 Iveagh Buildings: originally built for Dublin's poor by the Earl of Iveagh, close to St Patrick's Cathedral
24 mountains: Po Chu-I wrote a poem called 'Madly Singing in the Mountains'
27 populous: crowded/having a large population and
27 tangled: confused and complicated

Questions

1. What did you think of when you read the words 'Madly Singing in the City'?

2. The speaker here, having finished writing a new poem, takes some time out. What happens?

3. What does this poem say about the writing of poetry and how it comes about?

4. How does the poet describe the relationship between himself and the people he thinks about [the sleeping citizens] and sees [the 'restless ones'] from the roof garden?

5. Why does line six ['Fumes rise from the chip-shop] mark a turning point in the poem?

6. This is a poem that contains a sensuous description of fish and chips. Read lines 6-15 again. Do you think the poet paints a clear picture here? Give reasons for your answer.

7. By line 16 'the new words' are 'ready'. Explain what, in your view, is meant by this?

8. He says that, 'in a second', he will 'sing'. How does he explain what happens? Consider, especially, the line 'it will be as if/ a god has leaned with me'. What does this reveal about the poet's understanding of making poetry?

9. Do you think the speaker likes living in the city, 'in the roar of streets'?

10. What has happened by the end of the poem?

11. There are different kinds of singing here. Explain.

Critical Commentary

A man, having written a poem, climbs up to a roof garden late at night. He looks out over the city 'in the small hours', the smell from the Fish and Chip shop reminds him of being in the Chipper and the experience prompts him to find new words and make a new poem. The creative process is described in terms of a god-like activity in that the speaker senses that a god from the local churches has leaned with him over the railings on the roof garden and into the night and made possible another poem.

'Madly Singing in the City' begins with the poet telling us that he has just finished a poem, then there is the poem that we are reading and it ends with a sense of yet another poem about to begin.

The fact that this poem acknowledges and remembers a poem from Ninth-Century China creates a connection between poetry from another time, another place. It creates a link between poets, in this instance a poet living in Twentieth/Twenty-first century Ireland and a Chinese poet born over a thousand years ago. The Chinese poet Po Chü-I may never have been in a fish and chipper and he probably is not familiar with Christian churches but what connects people everywhere, in every time and in every place is our ability to respond to the situation we find ourselves in, what we make of here and now.

The speaker at the beginning of this poem is alone. He looks out over a Dublin in which some are sleeping and some are in the streets, 'restless' and 'shouting their tune/ in the small hours'. The poem is finished and he sees it as news 'for the sleeping citizens/ and these restless ones.'

Lines 6-15 describe the speaker's memory of being in the chip-shop, an ordinary, everyday place. The details allow the reader to see, smell, feel, hear, taste the experience. The writing here is clear, straightforward, sensuous. Then at line 16 the poem moves into another area of experience. He is thinking about 'the new words', words shaped into poetry. The local churches, seen from his house, are listed. These symbolise centuries of tradition and belief and their silent presences contrast with the restless people in the street, shouting, in the small hours.

The Myra Glass Company premises reminds him of the time 'we carried the glass table-top', another detail, like the chip-shop, from his day-to-day life. The speaker then turns to a deeper, more philosophical frame of mind and he is aware that he will sing his thoughts and feelings into poetry.

The speaker in the closing lines speaks of a form of divine inspiration. He knows that when he makes his song 'it will be as if/ a god has leaned with me, having strolled over/ from either of the two cathedrals, or from the green/ and godly domes of Iveagh Buildings'. The fact that he speaks of both sacred and non-sacred buildings as 'godly' creates an interesting connection. Inspiration can be found, it would seem, in a holy, sacred place such as a church but also in a less obvious place such as buildings that house ordinary people. That the god he mentioned has 'strolled over' creates a very relaxed and attractive feeling. The god has come to him to help his inspiration.

At line 24 he offers a biographical detail that might be true of the speaker or Po Chü-I or both. 'Ever since I was banished from the mountains . . . ' is a phrase that sounds as if it belongs to long ago. [Po Chu-i wrote a poem called 'Madly Singing in the mountains']. But the description of living in the city could be both old and modern. The speaker here reflects on what it is to live 'in the roar of the streets'. He learns about himself, he continues learning about himself and the words 'populous and tangled' that he uses to describe himself suggest that he contains multitudes, complexities.

The speaker's lungs, in the closing lines, swell 'with the new poem'. Once again, it is all about to begin. He has drunk in the city scene at night before him and from it he will make a new poem. In the opening line he is climbing up, having finished a poem; in the closing line he is going 'back down' to make another one.

His lungs are ready to breathe out the new poem. When he says that he goes down 'without saying a word' we know that he is ready with words and we've just read his other words that tell us he isn't saying a word. This becomes an interesting play on language and silence.

William Stafford   (1914 – 1993)

William Stafford was born in Hutchinson, Kansas on 17 January 1914, grew up during the Depression and graduated from the University of Kansas and later was awarded a doctorate by the University of Iowa. During World War II he was a conscientious objector and worked in the Civilian Public Service camps run by the Church of the Brethern. His work involved forestry and soil conservation in Arkansas, California and Illinois. He wrote about this in a memoir *Down in My Heart* [1947]. He taught at Lewis and Clark College in Portland Oregon and during 1970-1971 he was Consultant in Poetry at the Library of Congress. *Traveling Through the Dark* , his first collection, was published in 1962, when he was forty-eight and it won the National Book Award. His poetry features the Midwest and Pacific Northwest landscapes and he published a Collected Poems *Stories That Could Be True* in 1977. In all he wrote almost 22,000 poems and published nearly 3,000 of them. He says that his poetry is 'much like talk, with some enhancement'. Stafford wrote every day, liked to get up at 4 a.m., kept a Journal for fifty years, and he wrote about ordinary things. In a 1971 interview, Stafford said: ' I keep following this sort of hidden river of my life, you know, whatever the topic or impulse which comes, I follow it along trustingly.' William Stafford died on 28 August 1993 and that very morning he had written a poem that included the lines "'You don't have to/ prove anything,' my mother said 'Just be ready/ for what God sends.'"

Traveling through the Dark

Traveling through the dark I found a deer
dead on the edge of the Wilson River road.
It is usually best to roll them into the canyon:
that road is narrow; to swerve might make more dead.

By glow of the tail-light I stumbled back of the car   5
and stood by the heap, a doe, a recent killing;
she had stiffened already, almost cold.
I dragged her off; she was large in the belly.

My fingers touching her side brought me the reason —
her side was warm; her fawn lay there waiting,   10
alive, still, never to be born.
Beside that mountain road I hesitated.

The car aimed its lowered parking lights;
under the hood purred the steady engine.
I stood in the glare of the warm exhaust turning red;   15
around our group I could hear the wilderness listen.

I thought hard for us all — my only swerving —
then pushed her over the edge into the river.

Glossary

3 *canyon:* a deep gorge
6 *doe:* a female deer
10 *fawn:* a young deer
14 *hood:* bonnet
17 *swerving:* change of course

Questions

1. Why do you think Stafford called his poem 'Traveling through the Dark'? Would it make much difference if he called it 'A Car Journey at Night'? Could the title have two meanings?

2. How would you describe the poet's attitude towards what he finds on the road in the first two stanzas? What words best express that attitude?

3. What problem does the poet face? Why did he hesitate? What do you think he means in the line 'around our group I could hear the wilderness listen.'

4. How do you think the poet felt about the experience afterwards? Give reasons for your answer.

Critical Commentary

The idea of a journey is a familiar and popular one in literature and a journey can be a life-changing experience. In this instance, the journey, described in Stafford's poem, is certainly a significant and memorable one. It is also a disturbing and haunting episode.

It opens with a matter-of-fact sentence. The speaker comes upon a dead deer on the road. The deer is at the edge of the road, the speaker could have continued his journey without stopping. The fact that he does stop suggests that he wants to make things safer: 'It is usually best to roll them into the canyon: that road is narrow; to swerve might make more dead.'

The speaker 'stumbled', the dead deer is referred to as 'the heap' – there is nothing elegant or dignified about the speaker's actions or attitude. The facts are stated:

> a doe, a recent killing;
> she had stiffened already, almost cold.
> I dragged her off

It is only then that the speaker discovers the most important thing:

> she was large in the belly

78

and the description of the driver's response to the deer changes significantly once the discovery is made that this doe is pregnant. 'My fingers touching her side brought me the reason' - the speaker discovers that 'her side was warm'. A dead doe, a live fawn within that dead body is a terrible image:

> her fawn lay there waiting,
> alive, still, never to be born.

Birth and death are side by side in the one body but the situation is impossible.

The poem's two shortest sentences sum up the speaker's dilemma:

> I dragged her off: she was large in the belly.

> Beside that mountain road I hesitated.

It is a bleak, dark scene. The reader shares that complex moment. What can be done? What should be done? are questions that the poem invites us to ask.

At line twelve we are within the speaker's mind – he is hesitating, he is wondering what to do. The poem's focus then shifts to the scene itself. The poem's second last stanza paints a picture of a car, a man, a dead deer.

The poet's use of 'our' and 'us all' are important. The speaker has to make a decision. It is a difficult one. Does one leave the deer at the edge of the road where the fawn will eventually die within its mother's body? Or will the speaker move the dead deer. By doing so the road will be made safer but the fawn will die sooner.

'I could hear the wilderness listen' suggests that the world of nature is aware of what has occurred. Man has killed a deer on the road. Now another man will kill the fawn within the doe's body but the poem's closing lines suggest a thoughtful, hesitating, sensitive awareness:

> I thought hard for us all – my only swerving –
> Then pushed her over the edge into the river.

The final line, if read on its own, seems cold, matter-of-fact but the poem has described one man facing a very difficult choice. 'I thought hard for us all' includes the speaker, the doe, the fawn. And it also includes the reader.

Dylan Thomas   (1914 – 1953)

Dylan Thomas was born in Swansea, on 22 October 1914, and was educated at Swansea Grammar School where his father taught English. He began writing poetry during childhood, left school at seventeen, having failed his examinations in all subjects except English, and worked as a reporter on the South Wales Evening Post, before moving to London in 1934 when he was twenty. He published his first book, *Eighteen Poems*, that same year. He wrote poetry, a radio play *Under Milk Wood*, short stories, prose pieces. In a Note to the *Collected Poems*, Dylan Thomas wrote: 'These poems, with all their crudities, doubts, and confusions, are written for the love of Man and in praise of God, and I'd be a damn fool if they weren't.' In all he wrote only ninety-nine poems, 'Fern Hill', of which there were, supposedly, three hundred drafts, being one of his most famous. He married in 1937, returned to Wales and settled there in 1949. He lived in a boathouse on the Taf Estuary and in his nearby shed wrote many of his famous works including. *Under Milk Wood* and 'Do Not Go Gentle Into That Good Night'. A flamboyant and charismatic reader of his own work, he gave several lecture and reading tours in the US. He died in New York City on 9 November 1953 from a condition caused, it is thought, by diabetes and chronic alcohol abuse. He is buried at Laugharne, Wales.

Do Not Go Gentle Into That Good Night

Do not go gentle into that good night,
Old age should burn and rave at close of day;
Rage, rage against the dying of the light.

Though wise men at their end know dark is right,
Because their words had forked no lighting they   5
Do not go gentle into that good night.

Good men, the last wave by, crying how bright
Their frail deeds might have danced in the green bay,
Rage, rage against the dying of the light.

Wild men who caught and sang the sun in flight,   10
And learn, too late, they grieved it on its way,
Do not go gentle into that good night.

Grave men, near death, who see with blinding sight
Blind eyes could blaze like meteors and be gay,
Rage, rage against the dying of the light.   15

And you, my father, there on the sad height,
Curse, bless, me now with your fierce tears, I pray.
Do not go gentle into that good night.
Rage, rage against the dying of the light.

Glossary

TITLE Good Night: death
5 their words have forked no lightning: the wise men's words have not created something dazzling, brilliant [?]
7 the last wave by: the last wave having gone by; it could also refer to the final wave
13 Grave men: serious men but grave, meaning burial place, is also intended perhaps
16 my father: Dylan Thomas's father was blind in his final years and here Dylan Thomas speaks to his father who was in chronic ill-health, mainly through heart trouble.

This villanelle, with its intricate rhyming scheme: aba, aba, aba, aba, aba, abaa, was written in 1951, when Dylan Thomas was thirty-seven. Line 1 is repeated at lines 6,12, 19 and line 3 recurs at lines 9, 15, 19.

In a letter written May 1951, Thomas wrote that the only person that he couldn't show this poem to was 'my father, who doesn't know he's dying'.

In Notes on the Art of Poetry, Dylan Thomas asked himself the question 'What is my definition of Poetry?' and he answered it as follows: 'I, myself, do not read poetry for anything but pleasure. I read only the poems I like. This means, of course, that I have to read a lot of poems I don't like before I find the ones I do, but, when I *do* find the ones I do, then all I can say is, "Here they are", and read them to myself for pleasure.

Read the poems you like reading. Don't bother whether they're "important", or if they'll live. What does it matter what poetry *is*, after all? If you want a definition of poetry, say: "Poetry is what makes me laugh or cry or yawn, what makes my toenails twinkle, what makes me want to do this or that or nothing", and let it go at that. All that matters about poetry is the enjoyment of it, however tragic it may be. All that matters about poetry is the eternal movement behind it, the vast undercurrent of human grief, folly, pretension, exaltation, or ignorance, however unlofty the intention of the poem.

You can tear a poem apart to see what makes it technically tick, and say to yourself, when the words are laid out before you, the vowels, the consonants, the rhymes or rhythms, "Yes, this is *it*. This is why the poem moves me so. It is because of the craftsmanship." But you're back again where you began.

You're back with the mystery of having been moved by words. The best craftsmanship always leaves holes or gaps in the works of the poem so that something that is *not* in the poem can creep, crawl, flash, or thunder in.

The joy and function of poetry is, and was, the celebration of man, which is also the celebration of God.'

Questions

1. What is the effect of the words 'Do Not Go' of the title and their repetition throughout the poem? What mood is captured by these words?

2. The poem's title is repeated four times within the poem. What is the effect of this?

Identify and comment on the other lines and words which are repeated in the poem. Repetition can be monotonous. How does Dylan Thomas avoid it here?

3. Wise men, good men, wild men, grave men . . . . What does the speaker say about each one?

4. How would you describe the speaker's tone throughout the poem. Does it change at any point? Why? Give reasons for your answer.

5. Does this poem, in your opinion, paint a grim picture of old age and dying.

6. In this poem a son is comforting his father. Do you think his father would be comforted by the poet's words? Give reasons for your answer.

7. Dylan Thomas saw himself as a 'freak user of words'. Is this evident here?

8. Though the speaker thinks that the dying of the light is inevitable, unavoidable what does his attitude towards it tell us about him?

9. Seamus Heaney says of this poem that 'through its repetitions, the father's remoteness - and the remoteness of all fathers - is insistently proclaimed'. Do you agree?

10. Compare and contrast this poem with Sharon Olds's poem 'The Present Moment'. Which one do you prefer and why?

Critical Commentary

This poem takes the form of a villanelle, a very strict pattern. There are only two rhymes in the entire poem and each of the five stanzas has three lines, with a concluding four-line stanza. Dylan Thomas in this poem is expressing very powerful emotions and Thomas gives those emotions even given greater force by shaping and expressing them within such a regulated and strict poetic form.

The poem begins an impassioned plea from son to father and this opening line is a repetition of the poem's title which lends it even more emphasis:

> Do not go gentle into that good night

Strictly speaking the line ought to read as 'Do not go gently into that good night' but Dylan Thomas achieves a greater effect by his use of 'gentle', in that 'gentle' is slightly stronger than 'gently'; it adds to the speaker's pleading tone. It might also suggest that his father was a gentle man but being 'gentle' now is not appropriate.

From the outset the poem achieves a great surge of energy, especially from its rhythmic pattern and its verbs. In the opening stanza 'Do not go', 'should burn', 'rave' and* 'Rage, rage' give the lines conviction and momentum and yet that same opening stanza rhymes 'night' against 'light' and death is seen as 'that good night'. This would suggest that Dylan Thomas sees death as natural, inevitable, but he is on the side of life and therefore is urging his father to resist death for as long as possible.

The poem addresses his father but this is only clear in the final stanza. The speaker first addresses old age in general and then stanzas two, three, four and five focus on different kind of men: wise men; good men; wild men; grave men. He urges these different kinds of men, he urges all men to

> Rage, rage against the dying of the light

The speaker is sympathetic. He understands that wise men will have accepted the reality of death but he also knows that , because their wise words have not created a brilliance to counteract the darkness, they will not accept the good night easily. The good men, remembering their good deeds and their worth, want to live, not give way to the dying of the light. Wild men lived a different kind of life but these too, who rejoiced in life, realise that their wild life cannot last and they too do not want to submit easily to death. The grave men who may be blinded can still see a blazing quality to life and they too 'Rage, rage against the dying of the light'. Each of these stanzas ends with the idea of darkness ('that good night' or 'the dying of the light') and yet each contains within it a sense of the possibility of brightness:

> Though wise men at their end know dark is right,
> Because their words had forked no lightning they
> Do not go gentle into that good night.
>
> Good men, the last wave by, crying how bright
> Their frail deeds might have danced in a green bay,
> Rage, rage against the dying of the light.
>
> Wild men who caught and sang the sun in flight,
> And learn, too late, they grieved it on its way,
> Do not go gentle into that good night.
>
> Grave men, near death, who see with blinding sight
> Blind eyes could blaze like meteors and be gay,
> Rage, rage against the dying of the light.

That this brightness has to be extinguished by death heightens the sense of loss which accompanies death.

The final stanza turns from the general to the particular, from descriptions of wise, good, wild, grave men to 'you, my father':

> And you, my father, there on the sad height,
> Curse, bless, me now with your fierce tears, I pray

With this intimate address the mood is immediately more personal and our knowing that Thomas's father was blind adds to the emotional impact of the poem. It is in this final stanza also that the speaker refers to himself in a personal way: 'my father' and 'Curse, bless me'. The relationship between father and son emerges as the most important relationship in the poem but his father 'there on the sad height' seems remote

'Do not go gentle into that good night' and 'Rage, rage against the dying of the light' each occurs four times in the poem and Seamus Heaney thinks that the use of repetitions here insistently proclaims 'the father's remoteness – and the remoteness of all fathers'. Both lines come together in the final stanza for added emphasis.

David Wheatley   (b.1970)

David Wheatley was born in Dublin in 1970. While studying at Trinity College he edited the student journals *Icarus* and *College Green*. He was the Friends Provident national Poetry Competition winner in 1994, was awarded the Rooney Prize and the Vincent Buckley Poetry Prize. He now lectures at the University of Hull. Speaking of a central preoccupation in his own work, David Wheatley quotes Wallace Stevens: 'Life is an affair of people not places but for me life is an affair of places and that is the trouble'. Wheatley laments the fact that 'the maps people use increasingly show only roads, car parks and shopping centres'. Wheatley has edited several books: *Stream* and *Gliding Sun A Wicklow Anthology* [1998] and *I Am A Crocus: Poems by Children from County Wicklow* [1998]; *James Clarence Mangan Poems* [2003] and *Samuel Beckett Poems* [2009]. His own poetry collections include *Thirst* [1997], *Misery Hill* [2000] – from which 'Chronicle' is taken – and *Mocker* [2006].

Chronicle

My grandfather is chugging along the back roads
between Kilcoole and Newtown in his van,
the first wood-panelled Morris Minor in Wicklow.
Evening is draped lazily over the mountains;
one hapless midnight, mistaking the garage door   5
for open, he drove right through it, waking my father.

The old man never did get to farm like his father,
preferring to trundle his taxi along the back roads.
Visiting, I stand in his workshop door
and try to engage him in small talk, always in vain,   10
then climb the uncarpeted stairs to look at the mountains
hulking over soggy, up-and-down Wicklow.

Cattle, accents and muck: I don't have a clue,
I need everything explained to me by my father.
Clannish great-uncles somewhere nearer the mountains   15
are vaguer still, farming their few poor roods,
encountered at Christmas with wives who serve me oven-
baked bread and come to wave us off at the door.

My grandfather pacing the garden, benignly dour,
a whiskey or a Woodbine stuck in his claw,   20
a compost of newsprint in the back of his van.
You're mad to go love in Bray, he told my father,
somewhere he'd visit on rare and timorous raids,
too close to 'town' to be properly Cill Mhantáin.

All this coming back to me in the mountains   25
early one morning, crossing the windy corridor
to the Glen of Imaal, where schoolchildren read
acrostics to me of 'wet and wonderful Wicklow',
and driving on down to Hacketstown with my father
we find grandfather's grandfather under an even   30

gravestone gone to his Church of Ireland heaven,
and his grandfather too, my father maintains,
all turned, long since turned to graveyard fodder
just over the county line from their own dear Wicklow,
the dirt tracks, twisting lanes and third-class roads   35
they would have hauled themselves round while they endured,

before my father and I ever followed the roads
or my mountainy cousins first picked up a loy
or my grandfather's van ever hit that garage door.

Glossary

Title Chronicle: the arrangements of events or dates in the order in which they happened
1 chugging: moving with a series of regular muffled explosive sounds
2 Kilcoole and Newtown: small towns in County Wicklow [Newtownmountkennedy]
3 wood-panelled Morris Minor:
3 Wicklow: 'the last of Ireland's thirty-two counties to be formed' writes Wheatley in his Introduction to Stream and Gliding Sun A Wicklow Anthology. In Irish, Wicklow is Cill Mhantáin – Mantan's Church.
4 draped: spread
5 hapless: unlucky, unfortunate
8 trundle: move slowly and unevenly
12 hulking: large and clumsy
15 Clannish: closely knit to the exclusion of others
16 roods: a measure of land approximately a quarter of an acre
19 benignly dour: kindly in a severe or gloomy way
20 Woodbine: a brand of cigarettes
21 compost: decaying pile
23 timorous raids: nervous rapid visits
24 Cill Mhantain: Irish for Wicklow
27 Glen of Imaal: an isolated and beautiful part of Wicklow
28 acrostics: a poem or puzzle in which the first letter in each line, when read vertically, form a word or words
27 Hacketstown: County Carlow – situated in the extreme north-east corner of County Carlow where the heights of the Wicklow Mountains extend over the Carlow border for a short distance
31 turned: changed religion
31 fodder: food [usually food for cattle but here the bodies are seen as "feeding" the graveyard]
38 loy: a digging instrument

This is a sestina [a song of sixes]. The sestina is a carefully and deliberately made poem: six stanzas of six lines and a concluding three-lined stanza. The final words in each of the first six lines are repeated at the end of the lines in the other five six-lines stanzas and the final three lines each contain two of these six words. Strictly speaking all six key-words should be the same but Davis Wheatley does not strictly observe this rule. In 'Chronicle' the six words at the outset are: roads; van; Wicklow; mountains; door; father.

Questions

1. What does one usually expect in a family chronicle? Are there aspects in this chronicle that you can identify with?

2. It begins with a description of the grandfather, then, there follows a description of the speaker's father. Give a brief outline of the poem's structure. How far back does this chronicle go? How many places are mentioned in the thirty-nine line poem?

3. Do you think it a strength or a weakness that six key-words [roads/van/Wicklow/mountains/door/father] are repeated [with some variation] throughout the poem? Give reasons for your answer.

4. In stanza one the poet paints a picture of his grandfather. What do we learn about the grandfather in these six lines?

5. The speaker's grandfather did not follow in the family tradition. Explain.

6. How does the speaker feel about his country relations? Which details best capture and explain those feelings?

7. What prompted the poet to write 'Chronicle'? See stanza five.

8. Explore how roads play an important part in the poem.

9. How would you describe the mood or feeling in the poem? Does it change? How would you describe the speaker's attitude to his family past?

10. If you were to write your own chronicle what details would you include? If you were to write your chronicle in sestina form which six words would you choose as important?

Critical Commentary

Here is a poem that focuses on family history, politics, religion, love, the past and the present. It's a poem with big themes from a very personal point of view. The poem combines lived experience, what the speaker actually experienced himself, and what he has been told about his family's past.

At line 25 the poet explains how and why the poem came about. He is driving in Wicklow, 'in the mountains/ early one morning' and this leads him to remember his grandfather driving the roads of Wicklow. He also remembers another car journey that the speaker made with his father when they visited his great-grandfather's grave.

But the poem begins in the present tense. His grandfather is portrayed as an interesting man. He was the first to have ' wood-panelled Morris

Minor in Wicklow', a car usually associated with a stylish individuality. That he also drove through a garage door at midnight suggests a wild, reckless streak.

The speaker's grandfather didn't follow in the family tradition. He became a taxi driver not a farmer and when the speaker visits him in his workshop he tries 'to engage him in small talk' and yet it was 'always in vain'. The speaker is clearly uncomfortable in his grandfather's company and when he is with his country cousins. He doesn't connect with '[c] attle, accents and muck'. They are poor but generous these great-uncles and great-aunts. They 'serve me oven-/baked bread and come to wave us off at the door'.

Bray, where the speaker's family lives, is not the real County Wicklow according to the grandfather: 'You're mad to go live in Bray, he told my father'. Place plays a very important part in the poem. The speaker has his pupils in a creative writing class respond to the idea of a 'wet and wonderful Wicklow'. Placenames are mentioned – Kilcoole, Newtown, Bray, the Glen of Imaal – and Wicklow are clearly important to the speaker's family. Even Hacketstown, County Carlow, where family ancestors are buried, is 'just over the line from their own dear Wicklow'. That these ancestors [grandfather's grandfather and father's grandfather] were once Roman Catholic but were buried as Church of Ireland is mentioned as fact. The speaker offers no comment.

Roads. Wicklow. Mountains. Father. These are key to the poem. Wicklow and mountains are to do with place; roads [back roads; dirt tracks; twisting lanes; third-class roads] represent man's presence and the word 'father' is the link with family and the past.

The poem is a quiet meditation on something most readers can identify with. There is a natural fascination with those who have gone before, the family line. Every family experiences change. The speaker here has gathered stories, information, anecdotes from the past and has knitted these into his own experiences of his immediate family. Past and present come together. There is not attempt to draw a conclusion, a lesson or a moral from all of this and the poem is the better for it.

Richard Wilbur   (b.1921)

Richard Wilbur was born on 1 March 1921 in New York and educated at Amherst and Harvard. He published his first poem when he was eight years old. While serving in the US Army during World War II, he began to write poetry. He published his first book, *The Beautiful Changes and Other Poems*, in 1947, reflecting his war service in France and Italy and his love for the landscape and architecture of Europe. Since then his publications include poetry, translations, books for children and essays. Wilbur taught at Harvard, Wellesley and at Wesleyan. In 1987 he was named Poet Laureate of the United States. He has won the Pulitzer prize for poetry twice, in 1957 and 1989. In 2004 he published a *Collected Poems 1943 – 2004*.

A Summer Morning

Her young employers, having got in late
From seeing friends in town
And scraped the right front fender on the gate,
Will not, the cook expects, be coming down.

She makes a quiet breakfast for herself.　　　　　　5
The coffee-pot is bright,
The jelly where it should be on the shelf.
She breaks an egg into the morning light,

Then, with the bread-knife, stands and hears
The sweet efficient sounds　　　　　　　　　　10
Of thrush and catbird, and the snip of shears
Where, in the terraced backward of the grounds,

A gardener works before the heat of day.
He straightens for a view
Of the big house ascending stony-gray　　　　15
Out of his beds mosaic with the dew.

His young employers having got in late,
He and the cook alone
Receive the morning on their old estate,
Possessing what the owners can but own.　　　20

Glossary

3 fender: mudguard [American English]
7 jelly: jam [American English]
11 catbird: slate-coloured North American having a call resembling the mewing of a cat
16 mosaic: patterned, glittering

Questions

1. How would you describe the 'young employers' as revealed to us in the first three lines of the poem?

2. The cook and the gardener are up early and at work. How would you describe the world that they inhabit?

3. The young employers are sleeping. What are they missing on this summer morning? How does the poet describe the summer morning? Of the five senses, sight, touch, taste, sound and hearing, list the ones used by the poet to bring the morning alive.

4. Comment on the idea of 'old' ['old estate'] and 'new' ['young employers'] in relation to this poem.

5. What, in your opinion, does this poem say about money, possessions, wealth?

6. Look at the poem's structure: The first line reads 'Her young employers, having got in late' and the final line reads 'His young employers, having got in late'. What is the effect of this?

7. Some things are priceless. Comment in relation to this poem.

8. Does this poem, in your opinion, offer a commentary on the class system?

9. Listen to the music and movement of the poem. Why do you think the poet chose a regular rhyme scheme throughout?

10. Does this poem, in your opinion, describe a spiritual as well as a physical experience. Consider, for example, the poet's use of the word 'receive'.

Critical Commentary

'The best things in life are free' is a well-known saying; this poem explores that idea. Many things about this poem is ordered: the careful, neat, five stanzas on the page; the stately, regular rhythm, the rhyme scheme; the work patterns of both cook and gardener, the mosaic of dew on the flower-beds. The one, out-of-tune, discordant note is that of the scraped 'right front fender' in line three. The damaged mudguard suggests careless driving or drunk driving or both and the life of the young employers described in stanza one suggests an easy, privileged social life.

The poem focuses on the unnamed cook and the unnamed gardener, separate, at their work, early in the morning. They do not abuse their position; they do not slacken their pace simply because their employers are having a lie-in.

The poet celebrates work, first hers, then his. Stanza two is suitable stately, ordered. Everything is as it should be; everything is calm and everything is in control:

> She makes a quiet breakfast for herself.
> The coffee-pot is bright,
> The jelly where it should be on the shelf.

The poem's movement or rhythm here is slow – each line is a strong statement, each line paints a vivid picture. The setting is the kitchen and then the poem moves towards a description of the garden. It is as if a camera is moving slowly from an interior to an exterior scene. We begin indoors and stanza two flows into the third stanza allowing the mind to picture the cook picture the gardener and the flowing lines match that flow of thought:

> She breaks an egg into the morning light,
>
> Then, with the bread-knife lifted, stands and hears
> The sweet efficient sounds
> Of thrush and catbird, and the snip of shears

The details here are striking. The cook breaks an egg into a pan or bowl but the poet's eye captures it differently and beautifully. The egg as it is being broken contains a glow of morning light between the raised cracked shell and the falling yolk and white. We see the egg, we hear 'the snip of shears' and with the sound of the clippers we are outdoors, watching the gardener at work.

Both cook and gardener are employees. They are not and never will be as well-off as their 'young employers' in terms of money. And yet the speaker portrays them both and separately as in tune and aware of the beautiful morning. They 'Receive' the morning and such a word not only suggests a gift but also a spiritual experience as in receiving a sacrament as in communion.

The employers are young; the estate is old. The new and the traditional are set side by side. The gardener looks at the 'big house ascending stony-gray' but the use of his here reminds us that there is a dignity and a sense of achievement to his work. The house is not his but it ascends

> Out of his beds mosaic with the dew.

There is no communication between cook or gardener but the opening

lines in stanza one and stanza five connect them ['Her young employers
. . . . / His young employers . . . .] as does their response to the summer
morning. The young employers will have missed what many see as the
best part of the day. The sensitive cook and the sensitive gardener,
ordinary working people enjoy and appreciate the riches of nature. The
detail 'young' is repeated suggesting that both cook and gardener are
older. Older and poorer, older and wiser.

In the poem's final line, Richard Wilbur uses two very similar words:
possess and own but in this instance there is a world of difference
between them. Possess means to have as an ability, quality, or
characteristic. Own means something belongs to someone. [A person
can possess a kind and caring nature; one couldn't own that.] The young
employers own the old estate, the stony-gray house, the kitchen, the
coffee-pot, the flower-beds, the shears but they haven't on this particular
summer morning experienced/possessed that natural beauty of early-
morning light and sunshine.

The poem's final line favours the employees, the workers. They are the
ones with soul; they are the ones who appreciate the morning; and that
experience can not be taken from them.

PART II
PRESCRIBED
POETS

Elizabeth Bishop

Elizabeth Bishop (1911 – 1979)

Elizabeth Bishop was born on 8 February 1911 in Worcester, Massachusetts. An only child, her father died when Bishop was eight months old and her mother, who became mentally unwell, was confined to hospital when Bishop was five years old; Elizabeth Bishop never saw her mother again. She was brought up by relatives, was sent to boarding school and attended Vassar. When she was twenty-one a small inheritance allowed Bishop to devote her time to writing and to travel. She visited Europe and she remained a traveller for the rest of her life. The titles of her books, *North & South* or *Geography III*, for example, reflect her preoccupation with place and travel. Elizabeth Bishop lived in New York and Florida and spent from 1952 to 1971 in Brazil. She survived on grants and later some university teaching and returned permanently to the United States in 1972, where she taught at Harvard and MIT. She died in 1979.

The Fish (1940)
The Prodigal (1951)
Filling Station (1955)

The Fish

I caught a tremendous fish
and held him beside the boat
half out of water, with my hook
fast in a corner of his mouth.
He didn't fight.   5
He hadn't fought at all.
He hung a grunting weight,
battered and venerable
and homely. Here and there
his brown skin hung in strips   10
like ancient wallpaper,
and its pattern of darker brown
was like wallpaper:
shapes like full-blown roses
stained and lost through age.   15
He was speckled with barnacles,
fine rosettes of lime,
and infested
with tiny white sea-lice,
and underneath two or three   20
rags of green weed hung down.
While his gills were breathing in
the terrible oxygen
— the frightening gills,
fresh and crisp with blood,   25
that can cut so badly —
I thought of the coarse white flesh
packed in like feathers,
the big bones and the little bones,
the dramatic reds and blacks   30
of his shiny entrails,
and the pink swim-bladder
like a big peony.
I looked into his eyes
which were far larger than mine   35
but shallower, and yellowed,
the irises backed and packed
with tarnished tinfoil
seen through the lenses
of old scratched isinglass.   40

They shifted a little, but not
to return my stare.
— It was more like the tipping
of an object toward the light.
I admired his sullen face,   45
the mechanism of his jaw,
and then I saw
that from his lower lip
— if you could call it a lip —
grim, wet, and weaponlike,   50
hung five old pieces of fish-line,
or four and a wire leader
with the swivel still attached,
with all their five big hooks
grown firmly in his mouth.   55
A green line, frayed at the end
where he broke it, two heavier lines,
and a fine black thread
still crimped from the strain and snap
when it broke and he got away.   60
Like medals with their ribbons
frayed and wavering,
a five-haired beard of wisdom
trailing from his aching jaw.
I stared and stared   65
and victory filled up
the little rented boat,
from the pool of bilge
where oil had spread a rainbow
around the rusted engine   70
to the bailer rusted orange,
the sun-cracked thwarts,
the oarlocks on their strings,
the gunnels — until everything
was rainbow, rainbow, rainbow!   75
And I let the fish go.

Glossary

1 tremendous: it may seem unnecessary to gloss tremendous but poets are attuned to the nuance of words and the dictionary is a vital companion for the reader of poetry. Tremendous not only means immense; more accurately it means that which excites trembling or awe from the Latin *tremere* to tremble, tremble at; awe-inspiring

8 venerable: worthy of reverence, aged-looking

9 homely: familiar or plain/ugly (in American English)

17 rosettes: rose shaped patterns – knots of radiating loops of ribbon or the like in concentric arrangement

25 crisp: firm

31 entrails: the internal parts of the fish

33 peony: a large showy crimson or white globular flower

40 isinglass: a whitish semi-transparent gelatin substance used for windows, originally got from the swim bladders of some fresh water fish

45 sullen: showing irritation or ill humour by a gloomy silence or reserve

52 leader: short piece of wire connecting fishhook and fishline

53 swivel: a ring or link that turns round on a pin or neck

54 five big hooks: Bonnie Costello, in her book *Elizabeth Bishop Questions of Mastery*, says 'Five wounds on a fish make him a Christ figure but the epiphany he brings the poet has nothing otherworldly about it.'

59 crimped: shrunk and curled

68 bilge: filth that collects in the broadest part of the bottom of a boat

71 bailer: bucket for scooping water out of the boat

72 thwarts: the seats or benches for rowers

73 oarlocks: a rowlock – metal devices to hold the oars, attached by 'string' to the boat itself

74 gunnels: or gunwhale – the upper edges of a boat's side

In a letter Bishop wrote: 'With "The Fish", that's exactly how it happened. It was in Key West, and I did it just as the poem says. That was in 1938. Oh, but I did change one thing; the poem says he had five hooks hanging from his mouth, but actually he had only three. Sometimes a poem makes its own demands. But I always try to stick as much as possible to what really happened when I describe something in the poem.'

Questions

1. Between the opening line, 'I caught a tremendous fish', and the poem's final line, 'And I let the fish go', is a detailed and interesting account of Bishop's response to the incident. How does the speaker feel about catching this 'tremendous fish'? Which words and phrases, in your opinion, best capture her feelings? Comment on Bishop's use of 'him' and 'he'.

2. How does the fish react when caught this time? How and why does the poet empathise with the fish?

3. Comment on Bishop's use of language. What is the effect of repetition? Which lines or images are particularly vivid? Discuss images such as 'ancient wallpaper' and 'big peony' and say what they contribute to the poem.

4. 'I looked into his eyes. . .' says the poet in line 34. What happens?

5. How would you describe the speaker's tone? Look particularly at lines such as '– It was more like . . .' or ' – if you could call it . . . '

6. What do you think Bishop means by 'victory' in line 66? How would you describe the poet's mood in the closing line?

7. Does the ending of the poem come as a surprise? Give reasons for your answer. Why do you think the speaker 'let the fish go'? What does this poem say about power and control?

Critical Commentary

Elizabeth Bishop loved Florida and settled in Key West, Florida, between 1939 and 1948. There Bishop discovered her love of fishing and, days after pulling in a sixty-pound amberjack, she began recording in her notebook descriptions which would later become part of her poem 'The Fish'. In Brett Millier's words, it is a poem of 'remarkable clarity and straightforwardness'. The form of the poem is the trimeter line interspersed at times by the dimeter. This is a form often suited to storytelling.

The fish of the poem is the enormous Caribbean jewfish which Bishop caught at Key West. Though the opening line is direct, 'I caught a tremendous fish', the adjective adds interest and excitement immediately. The fish isn't just described as 'large' or 'huge', though it is both. Instead Bishop chooses the more powerfully subjective word 'tremendous', meaning immense and something which causes one to tremble. That first sentence is almost matter-of-fact:

> I caught a tremendous fish
> and held him beside the boat
> half out of water, with my hook
> fast in the corner of his mouth.

yet it is 'my hook'. That detail, along with 'half out of water' (the fish is out of his element, between worlds) and 'fast', adds to the dramatic quality of the opening lines.

The focus shifts with the second sentence, line 5, 'He didn't fight', from Bishop to the fish, from fisher to the thing caught. Now we are told something about this fish and the personality which the poet attributes to it.

> He hadn't fought at all.

The fish submitted. The description of it as a 'grunting weight' is the first of many vivid pictures:

> He hung a grunting weight,
> battered and venerable
> and homely.

'Grunting', 'battered' and 'homely' (meaning, in American English, plain-looking) capture the exhausted and ugly state of the fish, but then Bishop's use of 'venerable' casts a different light on things. It means both aged looking and worthy of reverence.

Bishop is an extraordinary observer. The fish, once caught, is not just cast aside. She looks at it in great detail. Line 9 begins this thorough examination and observation of the fish:

> Here and there
> his brown skin hung in strips
> like ancient wallpaper:
> shapes like full-blown roses
> stained and lost through age.

Throughout the poem there is a very definite sense of Bishop as participant and observer: 'I caught', 'I thought', 'I looked', I stared and stared' but the poem is so much more than a matter-of-fact account of catching a fish. The fish intrigues her; it fascinates and frightens her, teaching her something about the fish and something about herself.

The simile in line 14, 'like full-blown roses', is a beautiful image, even if the shapes on the fish are 'stained and lost through age'. Here the fish becomes less 'homely' but, as Bishop looks more closely, a less attractive aspect of this fish is revealed:

> He was speckled with barnacles,
> fine rosettes of lime,
> and infested
> with tiny white sea-lice,
> and underneath two or three
> rags of green weed hung down.

These physical details are such that the texture (speckled, infested, rags) and the colours (lime, white, green) vividly help to create the complete picture.

The fish exists between the two elements of air and water: 'his gills were breathing in/the terrible oxygen'. The fish will die if its gills drink in the air, not water, and the gills are 'frightening': they are 'fresh and crisp with blood', they 'can cut so badly'.
In line 27 there is a shift in emphasis signalled by the phrase 'I thought'. Here Bishop imagines the insides of the fish, that aspect of the fish invisible to the fisherman or fisherwoman. By speaking now of

> the coarse white flesh
> packed in like feathers,
> the big bones and the little bones,
> the dramatic reds and blacks
> of his shiny entrails,
> and the pink swim-bladder
> like a big peony.

we have a sense of the whole fish, outside and inside. The image of the feathers, the use of 'little', the colours red, black and pink signal Bishop's sympathetic imaginative response.

The 'big peony' is a startling and beautiful image. The guts of a fish are not often viewed in this delicate, imaginative manner. And this peony image sends us back to line 14, where the fish's skin was also described in terms of flower imagery – the shapes of full-blown roses.

In some respects the fish is familiar – his skin is compared to 'ancient wallpaper' – but the fish is also 'infested', 'coarse' and 'weapon-like'. She admires him, but she also recognises something disgusting in the fish. Yet the fish is ugly only to the careless observer; Bishop recognises that the fish is beautiful too.

When, in line 34, Bishop tells us that she 'looked into his eyes', a more immediate relationship between the poet and the fish is being established. The captor is now looking straight into the eyes of the captive. The eyes of the fish are then described in typical Bishop style: a style which seems objective at first but is in fact a style which reveals Bishop's unique and subjective eye. First the eyes are described in terms of size, shape, colour –

> his eyes
> which were far larger than mine
> but shallower, and yellowed.

Then we are given more detailed imagery, the irises are

> backed and packed
> with tarnished tinfoil

and even this image is overlain with another image – the image of the irises

> seen through the lenses
> of old scratched isinglass.

The fish does not return her look, her stare. The eyes, we are told,

> shifted a little, but not
> to return my stare.

The fish not looking, not returning Bishop's stare, suggests the separateness, the independence, the dignity and yet the vulnerability of the fish. When the stronger captures the weak it does not mean that the weaker one surrenders everything.

As in much of Bishop's poetry, the writing is such that, as we read through the poem, it is as if we are reading her thoughts directly as they are being thought.

The use of the dash at line 43 (she also uses the dash elsewhere in the poem at lines 24, 49 and 74) suggests a considered, explanatory addition; it indicates Bishop's attempt at getting it right. She has spoken of how the eyes shifted slightly and then we are given the further explanation or clarification:

> – It was more like the tipping
> of an object toward the light.

'I caught' (line 1), 'I thought' (line 27) and 'I looked' (line 34) have already marked certain stages in the poem. Now, with line 45, we have a new development: Bishop tells us that

> I admired his sullen face,
> the mechanism of his jaw.

Sullen is not a quality usually or often admired, but Bishop attributes a resolute quality to the fish and senses a gloomy and unresponsive state. It is at this point that she mentions how she saw 'five pieces of fish-line', each one indicating a former struggle and unsuccessful catch. The struggle was powerful and determined, and the fish still bears the evidence to prove it:

> A green line, frayed at the end
> where he broke it, two heavier lines,
> and a fine black thread
> still crimped from the strain and snap
> when it broke and he got away.

Here the adjectives and the verbs achieve the convincing effect: frayed, broke, heavier, crimped, broke, got away – that of a long, determined struggle. This fish has had an interesting and vivid past.

Bishop is clearly impressed. She sees the hooks as victory medals, while the gut lines are like the ribbons attached to such medals and they form a five-haired beard of wisdom. The fish, personified, has survived the wars – in this instance the fight with the fisherman's hook.

Earlier in the poem (line 46), Bishop has spoken of 'the mechanism of his jaw'; in line 64 we read of the fish's aching jaw. Bishop has become more engaged with the plight of this tremendous, battered and venerable fish. There is also, of course, the sense of the fish as male, as conqueror – it has battled with the hook and won. Now it is well and truly caught, but Bishop, female, does not play conqueror, as the last line of the poem indicates.

All the details so far lead us to the poem's conclusion. The second last sentence begins with the line 'I stared and stared'. It is a moment of triumph and victory; Bishop speaks of how

> victory filled up
> the little rented boat.

Everything seems transformed. The boat is 'little' and 'rented': nothing remarkable there. The fish, however, was 'tremendous' and 'victory' seems to belong to Bishop for having caught the fish, but also to the fish itself for having survived five previous hooks.

She mentions no other person in this poem; Bishop, it would seem, is alone in the boat. One person in a little boat floating on the sea conjures up a small scene, but the feeling which she is experiencing is an expansive feeling, a feeling which begins within and spreads to embrace and include the very ordinary details of the boat. 'The 'pool of bilge', the rusted engine', 'the bailer', 'the sun-cracked thwarts', 'the oarlocks', 'the gunnels' are transformed. In the pool of bilge at the bottom of the boat Bishop notices where oil had 'spread a rainbow'. And that rainbow spreads everywhere

> – until everywhere
> was rainbow, rainbow, rainbow!

The poem's final line is one of the shortest sentences in the poem. By the poem's end we ask what has happened between line 1 ('I caught a tremendous fish') and line 76. 'And I let the fish go' is not surprising. The word 'and' suggests that everything has led to this conclusion.

Bishop's use of rhyme in the final couplet (rainbow/go; elsewhere in the poem she prefers to use internal rhymes) also adds to the mood of exultation with which the poem ends:

> – until everything
> was rainbow, rainbow, rainbow!
> And I let the fish go.

This is the moment of epiphany and revelation, a visionary moment. (An epiphany is an extraordinary moment of heightened awareness, insight and understanding.)

The poem not only describes the fish, but also tells us a great deal about Elizabeth Bishop. The poet Randall Jarrell admired this poem for its moral quality. The speaker sets out to catch a fish: it is a battered creature and in the end the fish is let go. The fish has escaped the hook five other times – the 'five big hooks' have 'grown firmly in his mouth' to remind us, but this time it is literally being let off the hook. Bishop admires the fish for its individual self; as David Kalstone observes, 'victory belongs both to the wild survivor and his human counterpart'.

Bishop's 'The Fish' can also be seen as an allegorical poem: in other words it gives us a narrative which can be understood symbolically or at a level other than the literal or actual one. It is but one of several poems by Bishop which Andrew Motion has called 'arguifying, Metaphysical and fabling'. Between that opening and closing line not only is there, in Craig Raine's words, an 'unhurried, methodical, humane' response to the fish but 'she pronounces a true but merciful verdict on our precarious existence'.

These closing lines can also be read as a reversal of the macho stance. American literature has memorable examples of the fisherman in search of the fish. Melville's great novel *Moby Dick* (1851) and Ernest Hemingway's *The Old Man and the Sea* (1952) reveal a man's determined and ambitious attempt to conquer. But this is not a poem about the fish that got away: 'I let the fish go'.

The Prodigal

The brown enormous odor he lived by
was too close, with its breathing and thick hair,
for him to judge. The floor was rotten; the sty
was plastered halfway up with glass-smooth dung.
Light-lashed, self-righteous, above moving snouts,   5
the pigs' eyes followed him, a cheerful stare –
even to the sow that always ate her young –
till, sickening, he leaned to scratch her head.
But sometimes mornings after drinking bouts
(he hid the pints behind a two-by-four),   10
the sunrise glazed the barnyard mud with red;
the burning puddles seemed to reassure.
And then he thought he almost might endure
his exile yet another year or more.

But evenings the first star came to warn.   15
The farmer whom he worked for came at dark
to shut the cows and horses in the barn
beneath their overhanging clouds of hay,
with pitchforks, faint forked lightnings, catching light,
safe and companionable as in the Ark.   20
The pigs stuck out their little feet and snored.
The lantern – like the sun, going away –
laid on the mud a pacing aureole.
Carrying a bucket along a slimy board,
he felt the bats' uncertain staggering flight,   25
his shuddering insights, beyond his control,
touching him. But it took him a long time
finally to make his mind up to go home.

Glossary

TITLE: The poem was originally referred to by Bishop as 'Prodigal Son'.
The Prodigal: A reference to the story of the Prodigal Son in the Bible as told by St
Luke, Chapter 15: A certain man had two sons and the younger of them said to
his father, Father, give me the portion of goods that falleth to me. And he divided
unto them his living. And not many days after the younger son gathered all
together and took his journey into a far country, and there wasted his substance
with riotous living. And when he had spent all, there arose a mighty famine in that
land; and he began to be in want. And he went and joined himself to a citizen of
that country; and he sent him into his fields to feed swine. And he would fain have

filled his belly with the husks that the swine did eat: and no man gave unto him. And when he came to himself, he said, How many hired servants of my father's have bread enough and to spare, and I perish with hunger! I will arise and go to my father, and will say unto him, Father, I have sinned against heaven, and before thee, and am no more worthy to be called thy son: make me as one of thy hired servants. And he arose, and came to his father. But when he was yet a great way off, his father saw him, and had compassion, and ran, and fell on his neck, and kissed him. . . . (King James Version)

TITLE prodigal: wasteful, extravagant

2 close: stifling, unventilated, oppressive

10 two-by-four: timber with cross-section, 2 inches by 4 inches

20 companionable: happily together

23 aureole: the halo or celestial crown round the head of a pictured martyr or divine figure

Questions

1. What immediately comes to mind when the words 'prodigal' or 'prodigal son' are mentioned? [Bishop's original title was 'Prodigal Son'.]

2. Look at how the poem is organised and shaped (metre, line length, end-rhyme). Can you suggest a reason why Bishop chose this form?

3. How does Bishop imagine the life of the prodigal son in the first section of the poem? Is it all ugly and hopeless? Give reasons for your answer and quote from the text to support the points you make.

4. What is the effect of the use of 'But' in lines 9, 15 and 27?

5. Comment on the significance of 'sunrise', 'star', 'aureole' and the Biblical reference to the Ark.

6. What is meant by tone? How would you describe the tone in the opening lines? Is there a change of tone in the poem?

7. How do you respond and how do you think Bishop wanted her reader to respond to line 21: 'The pigs stuck out their little feet and snored' (a perfect example of an iambic pentameter)?

8. Comment on Bishop's choice of adjectives: 'enormous', 'glass-smooth', 'cheerful', 'overhanging', 'companionable', 'slimy', 'staggering', 'shuddering' and the power of the last word in the poem. Write a note on any four of these.

Critical Commentary

It is worth asking at the outset why Bishop should be drawn to such a figure as the prodigal; she often felt like an outsider, someone away from home, and, like the prodigal son of the poem, she also suffered from drinking bouts.

The structure of the poem consists of a double sonnet and the irregular but ordered rhyming scheme is as follows: abacdbcedfeggf

A different sound rhyme and a different rhyming scheme is used in stanza two: abacdbecfedfgh. An identical rhyming scheme is used in the first six lines of each stanza. David Kalstone speaks of 'two nicely rhymed sonnets' and how the 'air of sanity' in the poem is what makes it frightening, 'its ease and attractiveness only just keeping down panic and fear'.

The poem, though based on the story of the Prodigal Son, chooses to focus on the lowest and ugliest part of that man's life – his time minding pigs. The ugliness and unpleasantness is presented immediately in the opening line: 'The brown enormous odor' captures the colour and the impact of the stench. This is the world he knows now. It is 'too close', too close for comfort, and so close that he does not judge. Not judging in this context could mean he has lost all sense of a world other than this one. It could also mean that this man does not judge – in other words, he is not thinking whether he deserves this life or not. Later there will come a time when he will judge it wise or judge it best to go home and ask his father for forgiveness, but Bishop is suggesting at this point that the world of the pigs is so overwhelming that he does not judge. The phrase 'he lived by' in line 1 can mean that the prodigal son lived next to this horrible smell or it could also be interpreted to mean that he lived by it in the sense that it allows him to survive. The presence of the pigs is there before us in the two details 'breathing and thick hair'.

The first part of the poem brings us within the pig shed. 'The floor was rotten; the sty / was plastered halfway up with glass-smooth dung.' The vivid ugliness of 'glass-smooth' is all the more effective in that 'glass-smooth' is more often associated with the surface of a calm, beautiful lake. That the dung is 'halfway' up the wall reminds us of its prevalence and liquid state.

Lines 5 to 8 focus on the pigs themselves, their heads, more specifically their eyes, their snouts. As everywhere in Bishop, the observations are exact: the eyes are 'light-lashed' and 'self-righteous'. Who gives the 'cheerful stare' - the pigs or the prodigal? The dash at the end of line 6 suggests that the stare belongs to the pigs' eyes and that the pigs even stare in a cheerful manner at the 'sow that always ate her young'. (The *always* is frightening). Whether it is intentional or not, the line (line 7) does prompt the reader to consider this sow's behaviour towards its offspring and the comparison between that and the subsequent attitude of the father towards his prodigal son.

The pigs follow their carer and, even though he feels sickened by it all, something eventually ('till' – line 8) in the prodigal causes him to offer a gesture of comfort or affection:

> sickening, he leaned to scratch her head.

In line 9 we are given a sense of the prodigal's meaningless life and secret drinking bouts but something else, something other, is also introduced. Bishop reminds us that there is a world beyond the pigsty. There is the sunrise, and the morning sun transforms the ordinary and everyday. In this instance the barnyard mud is glazed with red. Earlier in line 4 we read that the ugly smelly pigsty walls were glazed with dung; here the mud and the puddles are made beautiful by the sunrise and, seeing them, the heart seems to be reassured.

Such a moment of passing beauty sustains him in his suffering and loneliness and exile:

> And then he thought he almost might endure
> his exile yet another year or more.

The use of 'But' at the beginning of line 9 indicates hope. And Bishop also uses 'But' to begin the second section of 'The Prodigal', this time to signal a change of direction.

> But evenings the first star came to warn.

Perhaps Bishop is using 'star' here as a signal of fate or destiny. If it is spoken of in terms of warning then the prodigal is being told that he must act or make decisions. Then follows such a comforting picture of order and safety (the farmer tending to his cows and horses and seeing that they are safe for the night) that Bishop speaks of it in terms of it being

> safe and companionable as in the Ark.

Lines 18 and 19 give only some details of the inside of the barn in lantern light –

> beneath their overhanging clouds of hay,
> with pitchforks, faint forked lightnings, catching light,

yet these few details allow the reader of the poem to picture it clearly.

'Clouds of hay' and the words 'safe and companionable' suggest warmth and a dry place, a contrast with the wet, dung-covered pigsty where the prodigal works. Line 21 is one sentence. It returns us to the world of the pigs and gives us both their vulnerability – 'their little feet' – and their ugly side – they snored.

The farmer shuts the barn door and goes home, but Bishop, imagining the life of the prodigal, never speaks of him as having a home separate from the animals. The farmer's lantern is observed: its light 'laid on the mud' forms a moving or 'pacing aureole', and this interpretation of light on mud is similar to the earlier lines in which the early morning sun colours the mud and puddles. The lantern light becomes an aureole or halo and this too, like the glazed mud in stanza one, sustains him.

We are given another very vivid description of the prodigal at work before the poem ends. It is as if the time spent among the pigs is so long and the drudgery so great that Bishop returns to it again to remind us of its awfulness. With

> Carrying a bucket along a slimy board,
> he felt the bats' uncertain staggering flight

we are once again in the wet and smelly dark. The prodigal's private, inner self is spoken of in terms of 'shuddering insights'. We know from the Biblical story what he is thinking, what conclusions he is reaching. These insights are 'beyond his control, / touching him'. This is the disturbed, aware Prodigal Son. But Elizabeth Bishop does not give us a simple, quick ending. St Luke says 'And when he came to himself. . .'. Bishops charts the journey towards that difficult decision with words such as 'shuddering', 'touching him' and the final sentence in the poem. Here again she uses 'But' with great effect; it wasn't an easy and it wasn't a sudden decision:

> But it took him a long time
> finally to make his mind up to go home.

The final word resonates particularly because the word does not hark back to an obvious rhyme and because of what it implies within the poem as a whole. The loner, outsider, exile is returning to the place where he will be forgiven and loved. Our knowing the ending of this Biblical story adds to the poem's effect. However, our knowing that Bishop's mother was confined to a hospital for the insane and that Bishop herself grew up never having a home to go to also adds to the poem's power and effect.

In a letter to Robert Lowell, dated 23 November 1955, Bishop herself said that in 'The Prodigal' the technique was like a spiritual exercise of the Jesuits – where one thinks in great detail about how the thing happened. In another letter to U. T. and Joseph Summers, dated 19 October 1967, she tells of how 'The Prodigal' suggested itself. It 'was suggested to me when one of my aunt's stepsons offered me a drink of rum, in the pigsties, at about nine in the morning, when I was visiting her in Nova Scotia'.

Filling Station

Oh, but it is dirty!
– this little filling station,
oil-soaked, oil-permeated
to a disturbing, over-all
black translucency.   5
Be careful with that match!

Father wears a dirty,
oil-soaked monkey suit
that cuts him under the arms,
and several quick and saucy   10
and greasy sons assist him
(it's a family filling station),
all quite thoroughly dirty.

Do they live in the station?
It has a cement porch   15
behind the pumps, and on it
a set of crushed and grease-
impregnated wickerwork;
on the wicker sofa
a dirty dog, quite comfy.   20

Some comic books provide
the only note of color –
of certain color. They lie
upon a big dim doily
draping a taboret   25
(part of the set), beside
a big hirsute begonia.

Why the extraneous plant?
Why the taboret?
Why, oh why, the doily?   30
(Embroidered in daisy stitch
with marguerites, I think,
and heavy with gray crochet.)

Somebody embroidered the doily.
Somebody waters the plant,   35
or oils it, maybe. Somebody
arranges the rows of cans
so that they softly say:
ESSO-SO-SO-SO
to high-strung automobiles.   40
Somebody loves us all.

Glossary

5 *translucency:* shiny, glossy quality
8 *monkey suit:* dungarees, overalls
18 *impregnated:* saturated
24 *doily:* a small ornamented napkin, often laid under dishes (from Doily or Doiley, a famous haberdasher)
25 *taboret:* a low seat usually without arms or back / a small drum (the 'et' is pronounced)
27 *hirsute:* shaggy, untrimmed
27 *begonia:* plant with pink flowers and remarkable unequal-sided coloured leaves
28 *extraneous:* of external origin, not belonging, not essential
31 *daisy stitch:* a design pattern
32 *marguerites:* ox-eye daisies
33 *crochet:* knitting done with hooked needle forming intertwined loops

Questions

1. What details immediately strike the reader on a first reading? Is this a typical or an atypical Bishop poem? Give reasons for your answer.

2. Lines 1 and 6 end with exclamation marks. How would you describe the tone of the opening stanza? Dismissive? Cautious? Both? Identify the other tones in the poem.

3. How does Bishop convince her reader that the place is indeed 'oil-soaked, oil-permeated' and 'grease-impregnated'?

4. Bishop has been described as a very accurate observer. Where in the poem is this evident? Quote from the poem in support of your answer.

5. Choose any stanza from the poem and show how Bishop creates an inner music in her use of language. Your answer should include a discussion of alliteration, assonance, slant or cross-rhyme.

6. Discuss Bishop's use of repetition in the poem, especially the repetition of 'why' and 'somebody'.

7. Were you surprised by the final line in the poem? How is the line justified within the context of the poem as a whole? Compare and contrast this poem and its final line with Philip Larkin's closing line in 'An Arundel Tomb'.

Critical Commentary

'Oh, but it is dirty!' There is no introduction, no explanation. The title sets the scene and there is an immediacy in that opening line. The 'Oh' is spontaneous, the word 'dirty' given extra force with that exclamation mark. In this, as in many of Bishop's poems, we begin with a place and Bishop's description of it but, by the end of the poem, the experience has expanded to include wider, deeper issues. It is a poem that moves towards a wonderful and, in the end, a not surprising last line.

The place is black and glistening and disturbing because it can also be dangerous:

> oil-soaked, oil permeated
> to a disturbing, over-all
> black translucency.
> Be careful with that match!

That final line in stanza one – 'Be careful with that match!' – is very ordinary, everyday. It certainly isn't a line one might associate with the language of poetry, but poetry is the living, speaking voice of the time. This opening stanza combines a language that is exact ('black translucency', for example) with an equally effective the language which may seem throwaway or commonplace, but which in the context of the poem is perfectly right.

A masculine place, usually, the filling station is given a human and domestic dimension in the second stanza. Father and sons give the place a family feeling, as do details later in the poem such as the wicker sofa, the dog, the doily. The word 'dirty' occurs in the first three stanzas. The place is dirty, the father dirty, the sons dirty; the dog is a 'dirty dog'.

The dirt is fascinating. Every aspect of it is noted: the father's clothes are so black they resemble an

> oil-soaked monkey suit
> that cuts him under the arms

the 'several quick and saucy' sons are 'greasy'. 'All', Bishop tells us, is 'quite thoroughly dirty'.

Stanza three draws us in further with the question 'Do they live in the station?'

The comic books are the only things which seem to have retained their original, 'certain color'. Bishop's humorous eye suggests that the plant is oiled, not watered; the doily is 'dim', yet the plant on the doily-covered taboret fascinates her. The doily is improbable and unexpected, totally unnecessary, it could be argued, and it is dirty:

Why, oh why, the doily?

is a question both simple and crucial. The doily reminds us that there are such things as creativity, grace, manners; it is a gesture towards elegance. Filling stations are naturally oily and dirty, and we've already seen how the father, the sons, the furniture and the dog are filthy. The doily is not as fresh as the day it was made, but it was created to decorate and to enhance. It was also most likely embroidered and crocheted by a woman, which may be another interesting consideration. A woman brought something special to this place and it is a woman who is reminding us of this in the very act of writing the poem.

The cans of oil have also been attended to in a special way:

> Somebody
> arranges the rows of cans
> so that they softly say:
> ESSO—SO—SO—SO
> to high-strung automobiles.

Whoever embroidered the doily, whoever waters the plant, whoever arranges the oil cans, is a 'somebody' never named. There is, it would seem, always someone doing small, almost unnoticeable little acts of kindness or acts which reflect our ability as humans to care, to shape, to bring order or to create. They are not always named and they do not need to be named, but the world is a better place because of them. Andrew Motion thinks the filling station 'the small theatre for a degraded life which stubbornly refuses to give up the effort to decorate and enjoy'. No matter where we live, we try to make it home.

The oil cans so arranged say musically and comfortingly 'SO-SO-SO', which was, according to Bishop herself, a phrase used to calm and soothe horses. This little detail adds a further interesting perspective to the poem. 'High-strung' automobiles refers to the tension and busyness of the cars' occupants more than the cars themselves, but the 'so-so-so' is doubly effective in that it was once used to comfort horses and now the phrase is read by those who sit in automobiles whose power is often described in terms of horse-power. The word 'high-strung' is also applied to thoroughbred horses; Bishop is describing the cars in terms of horses. The last line is astonishing and wonderful and totally justified.

> Somebody loves us all.

It is a short sentence, a line complete in itself and gains the power of proverb. It is a wise, true, and marvellously comforting thought with which to end, all the more effective and powerful when we see how the dirty filling station, observed closely, reveals this truth and makes possible this insight.

Gerard Manley Hopkins

Gerard Manley Hopkins (1844 – 1889)

Gerard Manley Hopkins was born in Stratford, Essex on 28 July 1844 into a prosperous family; his father, an insurance broker, set up his own company and it is still doing business. Hopkins moved to Hampstead and attended Highgate School and, later, Balliol College, Oxford where he studied Latin, Greek and Scripture. At Oxford he was awarded a first-class honours degree and he also, while at Oxford, converted to Roman Catholicism against his family's wishes and was received into the Church of Rome at the age of twenty-two. Hopkins taught for a while and then underwent a rigorous training for the priesthood. He was ordained a Jesuit priest at the age of thirty-three and taught in several Jesuit colleges in England and Wales. He was appointed to parish work in London, Bristol, Manchester, Liverpool, Glasgow. In 1884 Hopkins was appointed Professor of Greek and Latin at UCD and lived at 86 St Stephen's Green. He did not like Ireland – in 1889 he wrote 'five wasted years almost have passed in Ireland'. He was ill, overworked and unhappy and he died on 8 June 1889. He is buried in Glasnevin Cemetery in the communal Jesuit plot. The first edition of Hopkins's poetry was published in 1918.

Spring [1877]
Inversnaid [1881]

Spring

Nothing is so beautiful as spring —
  When weeds, in wheels, shoot long and lovely and lush;
  Thrush's eggs look little low heavens, and thrush
Through the echoing timber does so rinse and wring
The ear, it strikes like lightnings to hear him sing;   5
  The glassy peartree leaves and blooms, they brush
  The descending blue; that blue is all in a rush
With richness; the racing lambs too have fair their fling.

What is all this juice and all this joy?
  A strain of the earth's sweet being in the beginning
In Eden garden.— Have, get, before it cloy,   10
  Before it cloud, Christ, lord, and sour with sinning,
Innocent mind and Mayday in girl and boy,
  Most, O maid's child, thy choice and worthy the winning.

Glossary

2 in wheels: randomly
2 lush: rich and juicy; sap-filled
3 Thrush's eggs: a thrush's eggs are blue; Hopkins imagines them as miniature heavens
4 rinse: cleanse
4 wring: refined/purified
6 glassy: lustrous/shiny
8 have fair their fling: (the lambs) enjoy freedom and rightly so or (the lambs) have a fine sense of unrestrained enjoyment
10 strain: note/melody; a trace, inherited quality
11 cloy: become insipid
12 cloud: darken
12 sour: become embittered
13 Mayday: the innocence of youth
14 Most: best greatest; 'most . . . thy choice' means your best choice
14 maid's child: Jesus, son of the Virgin Mary

Written during the Whitsun holiday, May 1877. Hopkins was living in the Clwyd valley at St Beuno's college in Wales. A Petrarchan sonnet with a break between octave and sestet.

Several lines in 'Spring' illustrate Hopkins's use of Sprung Rhythm. Line 1 has four stresses, capturing the rhythm of common speech:

> Nóthing is só beautiful ás spring—

Questions

1. Spring is beautiful in itself. Which details best convey that view in your opinion? How and why does the speaker also see it as symbolic?

2. How would you describe the poem's rhythm and how does the poet achieve that effect?

3. Hopkins used language innovatively. Pick out some examples of unusual and effective word use and explain why, in your opinion, he used language in this way.

4. What is the effect of the question at the beginning of the sestet? Do you think the poet's answer contributes to the overall effect?

5. How would you describe Hopkins's tone here? Does the tone change? Why does Hopkins mention 'girl and boy' in this poem about spring?

6. The first eight lines have been called 'description', the final six lines 'doctrine'. What do you understand by such a division?

Critical Commentary

This is one of Hopkins's most famous poems and displays what Elizabeth Bishop called Hopkins's 'emotional rushing effect'. There is no stopping the first stanza. It begins with a strong, powerful, ultimate statement, what Norman White calls 'a burgeoning sound, a hyperbole'

Nothing is so beautiful as spring—

and the lines that follow illustrate that beauty in a surge of energy, 'by an ecstatic scene of movements, shapes, sounds, textures and colour'. The decisive nature of the words 'nothing' and 'so' and the tone they create are convincing and the poem illustrates why Spring is the most beautiful of all. This poem was written in May 1877, when Hopkins was thirty-three, and, in Virginia Ridley Ellis's words, is one of those poems by Hopkins that says yes 'wholeheartedly to the resources and richness of natural beauty as it bespeaks and is sustained by divine beauty'.

There is an ecstatic tone throughout the octet and the rhythm is free-flowing. Hopkins's command of alliteration and assonance are very effective in line two, when he offers his first illustration of spring's beauty:

When weeds, in wheels, shoot long and lovely and lush

Commenting on the verb 'shoot' here, Norman H. MacKenzie says that the 'happy rapidity of movement is exaggerated (as in a speeded-up film), after the sluggishness of winter ' and lush, meaning succulent, juicy, captures a sense of new life. That Hopkins celebrates weeds, and not flowers for instance, reveals his ability to find beauty in the everyday. In 'Inversnaid' he writes 'Long live the weeds and the wilderness yet'. The weeds are described as 'weeds, in wheels' which is an interesting detail. The phrase may refer to the radiating leaves which are like the spokes of a wheel; it has also been interpreted to refer to the tall grasses wheeling in the breeze and the third meaning says 'weeds in wheels' means sprouting at will, spreading here there and everywhere without hindrance, from the Shakespearean use of the word 'wheel' which means 'to roam', 'to wander about'. But whichever meaning you choose, the line certainly conveys movement and energy and something unstoppable.

The imagery is both broad-ranging and precise. The reader is asked to picture the expanse of heavenly blue sky and then to focus in on the little thrush's eggs in the small nest:

Thrush's eggs look little low heavens

Here, in one line, the poet has created the tiniest detail and a panoramic view side by side and, for Hopkins, it is God their creator that connects one with the other. The poem, having focused on seeing the blue of the eggs and the blue of the sky, then focuses on the sound of the bird's song, in a line that seem to run on and on:

> and thrush
> Through the echoing timber does so rinse and wring
> The ear, it strikes like lightnings to hear him sing

But even the thrush's song is seen in visual terms when its effect is compared to lightning strikes, and 'rinse' and 'wring' are ringing sounds, echoing each other, just as the trees (timber) are echoing with the sound of birdsong:

A specific tree is then named and its leaves and blooms are said to brush the descending blue of the sky:

> The glassy peartree leaves and blooms, they brush
> The descending blue

The blue skies, in line 3, were compared to 'low heavens' and here again, in line 7, the sky is referred to as 'descending blue'. Heaven and earth are brought closer here; it is as if heaven is on earth, that spring turns the world into a type of Eden. From the particular and precise detail of the 'glassy peartree', Hopkins then offers a broader picture but an equally effective description of spring when he says

> that blue is all in a rush
> With richness

and the first section ends with a familiar image

> the racing lambs too have fair their fling.

In eight lines Hopkins has moved from earth to heaven and from blue sky down to earth again. The verbs create much of the poem's energy and power – 'shoot', 'rinse', 'wring', 'strikes', 'leaves', 'blooms', 'brush' and the abundance and joy and freedom of spring are captured in 'long and lovely and lush', 'echoing', 'lightnings', 'rush with richness', 'racing lambs', 'fling'. The end rhymes also belong to key words, which only adds to the effect: 'lush', 'thrush', 'wring', 'sing', 'brush', 'rush', 'fling'.

The Eden parallel is made explicit in the sestet. Hopkins asks a simple question, a question which sums up all that has been celebrated in the opening lines:

> What is all this juice and all this joy?

And the answer follows immediately:

> A strain of the earth's sweet being in the beginning
> In Eden garden.

But the tone and the rhythm and the imagery are strikingly different in the sestet. Each spring we are offered a glimpse of paradise, of the world as it was before man's Fall. The second section contains no evocation of natural beauty, no detail as in the sestet. Seamus Heaney thinks that the poem, structurally, is 'a broken arch'. The octave, capturing as it does the essence of spring, is 'description' and 'a delightful piece of inscaping' but the sestet is 'doctrine'.

The feeling of exultation, so wonderfully expressed in the first eight lines, gives way in the sestet to thoughts on how mankind has lost that original joy. The Garden of Eden is echoed each year in the coming of spring but Hopkins prays that an innocence and inner spring may be preserved in the young.

> Have, get, before it cloy,
> Before it cloud, Christ, lord, and sour with sinning,
> Innocent mind and Mayday in girl and boy,
> Most, O maid's child, thy choice and worthy the winning.

The words here have none of the musical sounds of the octave and 'cloy', 'cloud', 'sour' have negative, not happy, joyful, associations. There is an urgency in 'Have, get'. Mankind no longer lives in Eden; our lives are sour with sinning and Hopkins asks Christ to make possible a spring-like quality in the young. There is a conviction in that final line. Hopkins imagines Christ as a boy (and Mary as a young maid) and he prays to Christ to make possible 'an innocent mind and Mayday' in the young.

In the final line

> Most, O maid's child, thy choice and worthy the winning

'Most' means best, greatest and most thy choice means thy best choice, the best to be chosen by thee. In other words Hopkins ends with asking God to look after the young and to keep them innocent. Otherwise they will become 'sour with sinning'.

The movement of the poem has been from a celebration of the natural joy and beauty of spring to his regret that sinful mankind has lost a quality which is as fresh and as innocent as the season itself.

Inversnaid

This darksome burn, horseback brown,
His rollrock highroad roaring down,
In coop and in comb the fleece of his foam
Flutes and low to the lake falls home.

A windpuff-bonnet of fáwn-fróth   5
Turns and twindles over the broth
Of a pool so pitchblack, féll-frówning,
It rounds and rounds Despair to drowning.

Degged with dew, dappled with dew
Are the groins of the braes that the brook treads through,   10
Wiry heathpacks, flitches of fern,
And the beadbonny ash that sits over the burn.

What would the world be, once bereft
Of wet and of wildness? Let them be left,
O let them be left, wildness and wet;   15
Long live the weeds and the wilderness yet.

Glossary

TITLE Inversnaid: on the eastern shore of Loch Lomond in the Scottish Highlands
1 burn: small stream (Scots word) – coloured brown (darksome) by the peat/turf
2 his rollrock highroad roaring down: the stream roars downwards and rocks the stones in its bed. This particular burn is Arklet Water. It flows down from Loch Arklet and enters Loch Lomond near Inversnaid.
3 coop: enclosed space where water is hemmed in by rocks
3 comb: water combing, cresting over rocks with a 'roping' effect, to borrow a word from Hopkins's Journal
4 Flutes: this has been interpreted as an image from architecture - the fluting on pillars; also, the music associated with the sound of the flute?
5 fawn-froth: the beige or fawn coloured foam or froth
6 twindles: a word combining twists/twitches and dwindles?; twindles, according to Peter Milward, expresses the movement of the froth as it is blown about and forms into smaller bubbles. Norman H. MacKenzie notes that twindles is a Lancashire word and means doubling or dividing in half.
6 broth: disturbed water
7 féll-: fiercely
9 Degged: (Lancashire dialect) sprinkled
9 dappled: variegated, patches of colour and shade
10 groins: the edge of the stream's path
10 braes: hillsides
11 heathpacks: clumps of heather
11 flitches: brown fronds resembling thin strips of tree trunk; ragged, russet tufts
12 beadbonny: the mountain ash or rowan tree with its pretty bead-like, red/ orange berries (bonny is Scottish for pretty)
13 bereft: deprived of, robbed of

This is Hopkins's only Scottish poem and was written on 28 September 1881. In a letter to Bridges he wrote: 'I hurried from Glasgow one day to Loch Lomond. The day was dark and partly hid the lake, yet it did not altogether disfigure it but gave a pensive or solemn beauty which left a deep impression on me.'

Questions

1. Which words in your opinion best capture a powerful stream rushing downhill? Which words help you see the stream, hear the stream?

2. This poem can be divided into two sections – description and speculation. How does one lead to the other? Why? Give reasons for your answer.

3. 'Hopkins's poetry is noted for its ability to compress ideas and feelings and to express them effectively and succinctly.' Would you agree that this is true of 'Inversnaid'? Which other poems are relevant here? Give reasons for your answer.

4. Write down those words which recur in the poem. Comment on Hopkins's use of repetition and say whether you think it effective.

5. Do you think that this poem is a good illustration of 'wildness and wet'? Why?

Critical Commentary

Hopkins was thirty-seven when he briefly visited Inversnaid, Loch Lomond, Scotland, and the poem describes, in its language and rhythm, a fast-moving mountain stream. It celebrates the natural world but, unlike 'God's Grandeur', 'As kingfishers catch fire', 'Spring', 'The Windhover' and 'Pied Beauty', this poem celebrates the creation without referring to God the creator.

The whole poem can be summed up in the final two lines and the impact which the stream has had on Hopkins leads him to this conclusion. From the opening word the poem achieves an immediate and vivid quality:

> This darksome burn, horseback brown,
> His rollrock highroad roaring down

This immediacy is sustained throughout as Hopkins conjures the various aspects of the stream, at times rushing furiously, at times darkly circling in its pool. At the outset, 'His' is used instead of 'Its', and personifying the gushing, powerful water indicates a strong involvement between poet and place. In a letter about his visit to Loch Lomond, Hopkins wrote that 'The day was dark and partly hid the lake, yet it did not altogether disfigure it but gave a pensive or solemn beauty which left a deep impression on me'. The darkness is found in the poem. The colours are sombre – 'brown', 'foam', 'fawn-froth', 'pitchblack' – for the most part.

Hopkins's verbal skills are clearly seen in the details. He chooses the Scots word 'burn' not stream and in one line the stream has become a brown-backed, galloping horse, a stream that rolls rocks down its course and roars; it moves even faster when the stream's course is narrowed by rocks, until eventually it reaches its home in the lake. Norman H. MacKenzie sums up these lines as follows: 'this is a wild horse . . . and the lather from his foaming flanks rushes under cooping overhangs and, combed into fluted grooves by rocky ridges, falls at last peacefully into its destined lake.'

Stanza two describes a pitchblack pool formed on its course, a hellish place suggested by 'broth' and 'pitchblack'. The water in the pool is like the broth in a cauldron and its movement so hypnotic that Despair itself (or a person in despair) would drown itself here.

> Degged with dew, dappled with dew
> Are the groins of the braes that the brook treads through,
> Wiry heathpacks, flitches of fern,
> And the beadbonny ash that sits over the burn.

Here in the third stanza there is a different atmosphere, one of freshness and delicacy, as Hopkins describes the upper part of the stream and its banks. It is no longer called a burn but a 'brook' and the water treads its way though the 'groins of the braes'. The colours here are more varied than in the first two stanzas – heather and fern and the 'beadbonny ash' (mountain-ash trees, with their bead-like scarlet or orange berries, growing along the bank). The image of the mountain-ash tree sitting over the burn suggests a gentle, easy, relaxed mood, which contrasts with the sound and fury of the opening lines.

The poem ends with a question and a plea. Though written in 1881, there was even then a sense of a world that could become over-crowded. Hopkins clearly loves this wild and wet landscape:

> What would the world be, once bereft
> Of wet and of wildness? Let them be left,
> O let them be left, wildness and wet;
> Long live the weeds and the wilderness yet.

The repetition is deliberate and effective: 'wet', 'wildness', 'let them be left'; end-rhymes and internal rhymes knit the stanza together into an urgent and heartfelt prayer.

Hopkins is not only thinking of a particular place but how everyone, everywhere, throughout the world, needs the wild expanse of nature to enrich and restore. Wildness is essential and even the weeds are to be cherished. He praised them in 'Spring' – 'when weeds in wheels shoot long and lovely and lush' – and he praises them here.

ptance

paradox

...ing us to him self

Christ died at 33

Jesus Christ fulfilled the

Thomas Kinkella

Contrasts him self with

It Deeply thought

Thomas Kinsella

Thomas Kinsella (b.1928)

Thomas Kinsella was born in Dublin on 4 May 1928 and 'The childhood event that had the most profound effect on Kinsella's later poetic outlook was living through the Second World War as a teenager and viewing its disastrous effect upon the world'. He wrote his first poem at eighteen 'out of curiosity' and his second, when he was twenty, 'as a joke'. Having abandoned a science degree at University College Dublin, he joined the Irish Civil Service but returned to UCD later as a night student and was awarded an arts degree. He published his first collection *The Starlit Eye* in 1952, when he was twenty-four. In 1965 he left the Department of Finance and taught at several American universities. In 1972 he founded The Peppercanister Press and published his own work under this imprint. He retired to Laragh, County Wicklow, in 1992 but he now lives in the United States. In addition to numerous collections, he published *The Táin*, a translation of Táin Bó Cuailgne, and edited *The New Oxford Book of Irish Verse*. His *Collected Poems* 1956 – 1994 was published by Oxford University Press in 2000.

Thinking of Mr D. [1958]
Mirror in February [1962]

Thinking of Mr D.

[handwritten: This is Thomas image of D when hes dead]

A man still light of foot, but ageing, took
An hour to drink his glass, his quiet tongue
Danced to such cheerful slander.

He sipped and swallowed with a scathing smile,
Tapping a polished toe.   5
His sober nod withheld assent. *[handwritten: Mysterious Man.]*

When he died I saw him twice. *[handwritten: Vision]*
Once as he used retire
On one last murmured stabbing little tale
From the right company, tucking in his scarf.   10

And once down by the river, under wharf- *[handwritten: where ship are loaded and unloaded]*
Lamps that plunged him in and out of light,
A priestlike figure turning, wolfish-slim, *[handwritten: Suggest Someone set apart.]*
Quickly aside from pain, in a bodily plight,
To note the oiled reflections chime and swim.   15
[handwritten: Difficult Situation.]

[handwritten: A Solitary Figure]

Glossary

'Thinking of Mr D.' was originally, in earlier versions, twenty-nine lines long, forty
lines long, and was not divided into stanzas. In the earlier version Mr D. was
described as 'A barren Dante leaving us for hell' [Dante – the medieval Italian poet
who in The Inferno describes his journey to Hell]

3 slander: a false spoken statement about another person [if such a
statement is written or printed it is called libel]
4 scathing: harsh, severely critical, scornful
6 withheld assent: refused agreement
11/12 wharf-lamps: the lights along a place where ships are loaded and unloaded
14 plight: a dangerous or difficult situation
15 chime: harmonise

Questions

1. What details does the speaker remember about Mr D.? Identify physical details and then aspects of his personality.

2. How would you describe the man portrayed in the poem? Do you think him an everyday, ordinary kind of man? Give reasons for your answer.

3. How can you tell that Mr D. was an important presence in the speaker's life?

4. How would you describe the moods of the poem? Which details best capture those moods?

5. Mr D. is described someone who entered into 'cheerful slander', as someone 'with a scathing smile', 'priestlike' and 'wolfish-slim'. What do these qualities add up to in your mind? Are they contradictory?

6. The phrase 'in a bodily plight' means an unfortunate state or condition and one of the poem's final image is of Mr D. 'in a bodily plight'. Is that the lasting, enduring image of Mr D. as he is portrayed in the poem or are other details more memorable in your opinion? Give reasons for your answer.

7. The poem's third and fourth stanzas are set at night and the speaker describes Mr D. 'in and out of light'. What is the effect of this in your opinion? Comment on the closing words 'the oiled reflections' that 'chime and swim'.

8. The poem is divided into four separate stanzas. Why do you think the poet chose to lengthen stanza three and four.

Critical Commentary

This poem remembers a man whom the poet found interesting and intriguing. The scene in the opening stanza is in a pub and the description is both physical – 'A man still light of foot, but ageing, took/ An hour to drink his glass' - and mental. He took his time to drink his glass and this deliberately measured action seems to reflect a calculating nastiness. He spends a great deal of time bad-mouthing others, all the while smiling his way through it.

Mr D. is just that. He is given no name, just an initial. Maurice Harmon says that the character of Mr D contains something of the poet Austin Clarke – Clarke, appears here, says Harmon 'as a sly reticent figure'. It has also been suggested that the medieval Italian poet Dante Aligieri [1265-1321] shimmers behind the poem. But even without this literary background information the poem stands on its own and stands alone. It could just as well be a about a family friend or neighbour.

The striking thing about Mr D. is that he's his own man. He does things his way, even in the way he drinks. He does not speak much. He can smile but it can be a 'scathing smile'. His shoes are polished. He taps a foot. He does not give approval easily.

All of these details are conveyed in the first six lines. These two three-lined stanzas are efficient and economical in their descriptions and yet they capture the mystery of the man. There is no getting to know a person fully; what Kinsella does here is that he offers some personality traits, some characteristics and the reader can build on these and understand something of Mr D.'s mystery.

The poem is in four sections, the first two stanzas focus on Mr D. when he was alive, in the last two stanzas he has died but he appears as a ghost. The lengthening stanzas [2x3; 1x4; 1x5] allow the speaker more room to dwell on the dead Mr D. and explore how he "saw" him twice since he died.

That Mr D. appears to the speaker proves his significance and importance to him. The two settings, a social gathering and alone at night down by the quays, also reveal his personality. In stanza three, the speaker imagines that he sees him as he leaves 'the right company', in stanza four he sees him moving in and out of lamplight down by the river. Again there are telling details that allow us to gain a better picture of him: He departs the gathering 'On one last murmured stabbing little tale'. That the hurtful tale is murmured is interesting; that he tucks in his scarf suggests a neat man. By the river at night he appears to the speaker as

A priestlike figure turning, wolfish-slim

and these details together create a complex, difficult-to-get-to-know man.

One of the most intriguing lines in the poem is the reference to Mr D., walking, alone, at night, and turning

Quickly aside from pain, in a bodily plight

No explanation is ever given. The reader is left wondering about the source or cause of this pain and difficulty. The mystery remains and the poem's closing line shifts to an image of the reflections on the river. The speaker imagines the solitary Mr D. looking at these reflections and reflecting. The 'oiled reflections' suggest an industrial scene by the river but the poem's final words 'chime and swim' create a lyrical and beautiful touch.There is in those final lines a reminder that there is no avoiding pain and suffering. Mr D. is something of a loner, an outsider; he has experienced 'bodily plight' but, even then, there are moments that bring relief, comfort, release. In this instance the beauty found in the most ordinary of places – the 'oiled reflections' – remind us of that.

Mirror in February

Month of renewed growth.

O = Opposite to whats expected in spring.

The day dawns with scent of must and rain,
Ready for planting
Of opened soil, dark trees, dry bedroom air.
Under the fading lamp, half dressed — my brain
Idling on some compulsive fantasy —
I towel my shaven jaw and stop, and stare,   5
Riveted by a dark exhausted eye,   *Realizes he's getting older.*
A dry downturning mouth.

A mood of Acceptance
It seems again that it is time to learn,   *paradox.*
In this untiring, crumbling place of growth
To which, for the time being, I return.   10
Now plainly in the mirror of my soul *looking inside himself.*
I read that I have looked my last on youth
And little more; for they are not made whole
That reach the age of Christ. *Christ died at 33.*

Below my window the awakening trees,   15
Hacked clean for better bearing, stand defaced
Suffering their brute necessities, *Harsh treatment.*
And how should the flesh not quail that span for span
Is mutilated more? In slow distaste
I fold my towel with what grace I can,   20
Not young and not renewable, but man.

A note of Acceptance.

Jesus Christ forfilled his purpose in life but Thomas Kinsella hasnt.

He Contrasts himSelf with 1) christ 2) trees outside.

A Deeply thought provoking poem.

135

Glossary

1 must: mould

3/4 my brain/ Idling on some compulsive fantasy: my brain lingering on some compelling/irresistible imagined idea

6 Riveted: held fast/fixed

13/14 they are not made whole/ That reach the age of Christ: Christ died at thirty-three, an age that is said to be the age of perfection. It is also said that when Christians on the last day are resurrected, their souls will be re-united with their thirty-three year old bodies, regardless of the age at which they died. Everyone in heaven therefore, supposedly, is thirty-three

16 Hacked: cut back with rough blows

18 quail: shrink back/ flinch

19 mutilated: maim, deform [and a verb which Seamus Deane notes as 'highly characteristic of the poet']

18 span: a stretch of time, especially of life

20 fold my towel: perhaps a play on "throwing in the towel"

20 grace: willingness, elegance, beauty

Kinsella himself says of 'Mirror in February': 'the preoccupation with age &c., is due to a combination of things: he has caught a hard look at himself in the mirror, is aware of pruning time in the orchard outside — and is thirty-three years old.... "and little more" — it is a harsh look in the circumstances; he is judging himself by high standards, the age thirty-three being a cliché, when associated with Christ, for perfection. "not made whole" suggests life is, or ought to be, a process of development, of growth toward something. In stanza three he senses the same organic process in all living things, as long as growth or development continues: man has more to expect, why shouldn't he expect to pay more?'

Questions

1. How would you describe the atmosphere in the poem? Consider the world within the room, the world outside. Which words, phrases, images, in your opinion, best convey that atmosphere?

2. What does the idea of 'mirror' suggest? What do you associate with February? Comment on the actual mirror and what Kinsella calls 'the mirror of my soul'.

3. How does the poet achieve a direct, immediate effect here? Consider Kinsella's use of the present tense - 'I towel', 'I read', 'I fold'.

4. How significant is the reference to Christ? Is this a religious poem? A spiritual poem? What do you think Kinsella means by 'grace' in line 20.

5. Why is the paradoxical image of an 'untiring, crumbling place of growth' central to the poem? Do you think the poem more optimistic or pessimistic?

6. The 'sensual' and the 'dramatic' are characteristic of Kinsella's poetry. Is this true of 'Mirror in February'?

7. Consider the words 'hacked', 'defaced', 'brute', 'quail', 'mutilated'. What do they imply?

8. Kinsella believes that personal survival depends upon the exploration of one's imagination. What do you understand by this? Is such an outlook reflected in 'Mirror in February'.

9. Examine the rhyming scheme. Look at lines 6-7 ('eye'/'mouth') and lines 13-14 ('whole'/'Christ'). Why do you think Kinsella ends the third stanza with a rhyme ('can'/'man')? What does such an ending contribute to the tone and mood?

10. Do you think one could tell that this is a twentieth-century poem? Kinsella is a city poet. How would you describe his relationship with nature? What kind of self-portrait emerges from 'Mirror in February'?

11. In *The Field Day Anthology of Irish Writing*, Kinsella's poetry is described as 'introspective and moody'. Is that true of this particular poem?

Critical Commentary

Poetry has been written for thousands of years but in English poetry the image of a man shaving himself before a mirror in the morning did not occur within a poem until the second half of the twentieth century. But it is not just this subject matter but its theme and way of viewing the world that makes this a poem of our time.

In the mirror we see ourselves at a particular point in time. Each time we see ourselves, time has passed and we are that bit older. Most times we look at ourselves for practical purposes but a mirror also allows us to become more serious, reflective.

The title contains 'mirror' but it also contains 'February', a time of renewal, growth, beginnings. The springtime of the year, however, does not bring with it the joys of spring in any obvious way. Kinsella's poem begins atmospherically, sensuously, dramatically:

> The day dawns with scent of must and rain,
> Of opened soil, dark trees, dry bedroom air

Dawn is frequently associated with hope and promise but here 'opened soil', 'dark' and 'dry' suggest the opposite. The earth is opened for planting but it is also opened for burial and the reality of growing old and dying serves as a backdrop for the poem.

The mood throughout is analytical and, in Augustine Martin's words, the poem explores 'universal states of mind: that moment between sleep and awakening when the individual looks at himself in the "mirror of his soul" and thinks about the passing of time, the process of ageing and the coming of death'. In stanza one the speaker presents an unflattering self-portrait. Words such as 'shaving jaw', 'Riveted', 'dark', 'exhausted', 'dry', 'downturning' are in sound and meaning awkward, harsh-sounding. And yet the phrase 'compulsive fantasy' stands out. The idea of his wild and extravagant imagination ('fantasy') contrasts effectively with the ageing body. Though it is early morning, there is no sense of the speaker feeling physically rested or restored after sleep but 'compulsive' suggests an energy and determination in his life.

Stanza two begins in a mood of acceptance: 'It seems again that it is time to learn'. With each new day and with the beginning of each new year, the human being is offered another opportunity to learn. The world is seen as a place that never tires, and, though a place of growth, it is also a place of decay ('crumbling'). Line 9 contains a striking paradox or apparent contradiction:

> this untiring, crumbling place of growth

This is the world the speaker returns to every morning. Sleep offers release and escape but dawn awakens the speaker to a new day.
There's a very straightforward honesty when the poet says:

> Now plainly in the mirror of my soul
> I read that I have looked my last on youth
> And little more

Here the mood is despondent, disappointed, melancholy. The mirror on the wall has become the 'mirror of my soul'. He is no longer looking at his physical self; he is now looking into his spiritual self. He is thirty-three years of age and he gently mocks the notion of thirty-three being the age of perfection. He sees himself, the physical and spiritual entity that he is, and wryly (with dry humour) concludes:

> for they are not made whole
> That reach the age of Christ.

The poem is set indoors and the poet looks inwards and examines the inner life but the glimpse of the world beyond the window in line 2 is revisited in the third and final stanza. The poet is troubled but he comes to realise, not only the inevitability of suffering, but also its worth. The trees are pruned, cut back savagely, but they are more fruitful as a result. Their suffering is brutal but necessary (the harsh sounding 'hacked' and 'brute' add to the effect).

The speaker accepts and suggests that the hacked trees are a symbol for man's life. He also accepts that man, who demands more than the trees from life, therefore has to endure more.

> Below my window the awakening trees,
> Hacked clean for better bearing, stand defaced
> Suffering their brute necessities

and the answer to his question is implied:
And how should the flesh not quail that span for span

> Is mutilated more?

The flesh does quail but it also suffers and survives its mutilations. Kinsella paints a realistic picture, not a pretty one. The disillusionment, lack of joy, tiredness have not disappeared; he still expresses distaste for life but he will go on:
> In slow distaste
> I fold my towel with what grace I can,
> Not young and not renewable, but man.

That the third and final stanza is the only one with a final rhyming couplet is significant. The rhymes 'can' and 'man' give the stanza a small lift, a sense of something vaguely upbeat. 'Not' is used twice and the negatives prevent the poem from arriving at anything resembling optimism: Not young and not renewable is a line that tells it how it is. However the use of 'but' in 'but man' strikes a tone of acceptance and resolve and the reader can recognise his/her own human condition in that final line.

Derek Mahon

Derek Mahon (b. 1941)

Derek Mahon was born on 23 November 1941 in Belfast. He was educated at the Royal Belfast Academical Institution, Trinity College, Dublin where he studied modern languages, and the Sorbonne. After college he travelled, worked as a teacher in Belfast and Dublin, and settled in London. For Mahon there are three principles essential to poetry: 'Soul, Song and Formal Necessity'. He published his first collection, *Night Crossing*, in 1968 and other collections include *The Snow Party* (1975), *The Hunt by Night* (1982), *Antarctica* (1986) and *The Yellow Book* (1997). He now lives in Dublin and says that 'solitude and community; the weirdness and terrors of solitude; the stifling and the consolations of solitude' are among his themes. What interests him is a poetry 'written by solitaires in the cold, written by solitaires in the open, which is where the human soul really is. That for me is where it really is.' He edited, with Peter Fallon, *The Penguin Book of Contemporary Irish Poetry* (1990) and his *Collected Poems* was published in 1999.

Grandfather
After the Titanic
Antarctica

Grandfather

They brought him in on a stretcher from the world,
Wounded but humorous; and he soon recovered.
Boiler-rooms, row upon row of gantries rolled
Away to reveal the landscape of a childhood
Only he can recapture. Even on cold   5
Mornings he is up at six with a block of wood
Or a box of nails, discreetly up to no good
Or banging round the house like a four-year-old—

Never there when you call. But after dark
You hear his great boots thumping in the hall   10
And in he comes, as cute as they come. Each night
His shrewd eyes bolt the door and set the clock
Against the future, then his light goes out.
Nothing escapes him; he escapes us all.

Glossary

Title Grandfather: Mahon's grandfather worked in the Harland and Wolff
shipyard in Belfast
3 gantries: platforms for travelling-cranes
7 discreetly: unobtrusively; separately
12 shrewd: sharp, sensible

Questions

1. How was the grandfather affected by his injury? Do the details
'wounded' and 'humorous' suggest the usual or the unusual?

2. Do you think that the past is important to the grandfather, according
to the poet? What does he mean by 'the landscape of a childhood'?

3. What do the details in lines 5 – 9 suggest? Are they contradictory, do
you think?

4. Would you think the poet's grandfather a secretive man? A sly man? A
cautious man? A liberated man? Give reasons for your answer. In what
way is he like a four-year-old?

5. Does the final line of the poem – 'Nothing escapes him; he escapes us
all.' – sum up the man as he is portrayed in the poem, in your opinion?

6. Comment on lines 12 and 13. What do these lines reveal of the
grandfather?

7. Why do you think Mahon chose the compact, well-made sonnet form
for this poem about his grandfather?

Critical Commentary

Mahon is a poet who values traditional poetic forms and techniques such as structure and rhyme. 'Grandfather' is a sonnet, a nostalgic lyric, with a regular rhyming scheme in the octave (abba abba) and a less regular pattern of rhyme and slant-rhyme in the sestet (cd cc cd). The speaker is remembering how his grandfather survived an accident and injury but no specific details are given. He was brought home on a stretcher but the image of being brought in 'on a stretcher from the world' suggests a vast world beyond the house where the grandfather will now recover. His personality is captured in the two contradictory words 'Wounded but humorous' and these suggest a man who is capable of making the most of a bad situation; 'and he soon recovered' suggests his determination.

The 'Boiler-rooms, row upon row of gantries' in line three belong to the grandfather's world of work at Harland and Woolf, where he was a foreman. But the speaker imagines that the world of the shipyards fades away and his grandfather returns to his own private world of memory and childhood:

> Boiler-rooms, row upon row of gantries rolled
> Away to reveal the landscape of a childhood
> Only he can recapture.

Here the present is contrasted with the past. It is as if the 'Boiler-rooms and 'row upon row of gantries' represent a harsh, confining world, whereas the words 'rolled/ Away' suggest the magical, expansive world of childhood. His early years are referred to as 'landscape', thus highlighting a difference between the enclosed, mechanised world of work and the broad expanse and ease of boyhood, a private, unique world known only to the poet's grandfather.

For the remainder of the poem Mahon describes his grandfather pottering around the house, his habits and his personality. The poet moves from dawn to dusk - he is up at six and busy, and at night he secures the house. He is happy to repair and mend and to make a noise – 'banging round the house like a four-year-old' – and is cautious and careful after dark, ensuring that the door is bolted and the clock wound. And yet the speaker makes several references to his grandfather's elusive, "unget-at-able", mysterious self. He is 'Never there when you call'; he is 'as cute as they come' and though

> Nothing escapes him; he escapes us all.

Though very much a definite and noisy presence ('banging', 'thumping'), he is nonetheless difficult to pin down. When he goes to sleep 'his light goes out' but there's an energy within him that seems to shine.
The poem celebrates the mystery of the individual and the fact that the individual, in this instance, is an ordinary man in an ordinary place reminds us that everyone is individual, mysterious in one's own way.

After the Titanic

They said I got away in a boat
And humbled me at the inquiry. I tell you
    I sank as far that night as any
Hero. As I sat shivering on the dark water
    I turned to ice to hear my costly   5
Life go thundering down in a pandemonium of
    Prams, pianos, sideboards, winches,
Boilers bursting and shredded ragtime. Now I hide
    In a lonely house behind the sea
Where the tide leaves broken toys and hatboxes   10
    Silently at my door. The showers of
April, flowers of May mean nothing to me, nor the
    Late light of June, when my gardener
Describes to strangers how the old man stays in bed
    On seaward mornings after nights of   15
Wind, takes his cocaine and will see no one. Then it is
    I drown again with all those dim
Lost faces I never understood, my poor soul
    Screams out in the starlight, heart
Breaks loose and rolls down like a stone.   20
    Include me in your lamentations.

Glossary

Title After the Titanic: an earlier version of this poem was called 'Bruce Ismay's Soliloquy'. Bruce Ismay was manager of the White Star Line. The Titanic, which was built in Belfast, sank on its maiden voyage from Southampton to New York on the night of 14 April 1912 at 11.40 p.m. The British White Star liner Titanic, measuring 882 feet 9 inches and 100 feet high to the bridge level, was the largest ship afloat. It cost £1,500,000. The Titanic collided with an iceberg in the North Atlantic and sank in less than three hours; c.1550 of c. 2206 passengers died. J. Bruce Ismay was 49 at the time of the disaster. Robert Ballard, in *The Discovery of the Titanic,* writes that 'Bruce Ismay, the wealthy president and managing director of International Mercantile Marine, which owned the White Star Line, had hopped into the partly filled collapsible C [lifeboat] as it was about to be lowered away, and lived to regret his instinct for survival. After his public vilification as J. "Brute" Ismay, he became a recluse and eventually died a broken man.'
2 inquiry: from 2 May to 3 July 1912 the British Board of Trade Inquiry was conducted; 25,622 questions were asked of 96 witnesses. There were only three passenger witnesses - Sir Cosmo and Lady Duff Gordon and J. Bruce Ismay
6 pandemonium: uproar, utter confusion; literally all (pan) demons, the home of demons
7 winches: hoisting machines

8 ragtime: music of American Negro origin; during the sinking of the Titanic the band began to play lively ragtime tunes

16 cocaine: drug from coca, a Latin American shrub, used as anaesthetic or stimulant

21 lamentations: expressions of grief, mourning

Questions

1. Why do you think Derek Mahon wrote 'After the Titanic'? Do you think it a more effective title than the original one, 'Bruce Ismay's Soliloquy'? Give reasons for your answer.

2. How would you describe Bruce Ismay's life after the Titanic? How does the poem convey loneliness and misery?

3. Does this poem succeed in making you view the Titanic disaster differently? Why?

4. How does the speaker here view the other passengers on the Titanic? Quote from the poem to support your answer.

5. Comment on the line 'I turned to ice'. Why is it particularly effective in this instance?

6. How is nature portrayed in this poem? Look at phrases such as 'the tide leaves broken toys,' 'flowers of May,' 'Late light of June.'

7. Eamon Grennan, commenting on this poem, says that Bruce Ismay delivers a 'distraught yet dignified' confession to the world. Would you agree with this description. Give reasons for your answer.

8. Consider the shape of this poem on the page. Most of Mahon's poems use a straight, left-hand, vertical line. Only eight poems in his Collected Poems (including 'After the Titanic' and 'Ecclesiastes') follow an irregular left-hand pattern. Why do you think Mahon opts for it here?

Critical Commentary

This poem illustrates what Eamon Grennan calls 'Mahon's belief in speech as value and as an epitome of identity'. In 'After the Titanic', Mahon does not speak in his own voice; he invents another speaker and the story of the Titanic is told from Bruce Ismay's point of view.

The speaker begins with how he himself has been viewed and treated:

> They said I got away in a boat
> And humbled me at the inquiry

and phrases such as 'got away' and 'humbled' suggest accusation and hurt. The story is well-known but Mahon has Bruce Ismay, with great economy, summon up again the terror and commotion of that night.

The cold night, Ismay's cold fear, the list of objects and the incongruous sounds of bursting boilers and jazz all create in five lines a sense of the disaster:

> I sank as far that night as any
> Hero. As I sat shivering on the dark water
> I turned to ice to hear my costly
> Life go thundering down in a pandemonium of
> Prams, pianos, sideboards, winches,
> Boilers bursting and shredded ragtime.

The 'I tell you' which introduces this confession is emphatic and pleading. Over one and a half thousand people died; Bruce Ismay was not one of these and yet he says that his life since is a living death. The poem then focuses on the present – 'Now I hide/ In a lonely house behind the sea'. Even though he hides 'behind the sea' there is no escaping his past. The sea itself keeps reminding him; the tide leaves

> broken toys and hatboxes
> Silently at my door.

Earlier 'Prams' reminded the reader of the children aboard the Titanic; here 'broken toys' achieve a similar effect, broken reminding us further of loss.

The speaker is unable to escape the past. The beauty of the natural world, spring becoming summer, makes no difference to him and he sees himself as others see him when he says:

> my gardener
> Describes to strangers how the old man stays in bed
> On seaward mornings after nights of
> Wind, takes his cocaine and will see no one.

The speaker, Ismay, does not contradict this bleak, drugged, isolated portrait of himself and he ends the poem with an image of reliving the torment of 14 April 1912. He suffers again and again and admits that he never understood 'those dim/ Lost faces' of those who drowned. The verbs are particularly effective at capturing his anguish – his soul 'screams', his heart 'breaks' and 'rolls like a stone'. The drowned that night cried out in their sorrow and lamentations. The poem's final line is the poem's shortest sentence and here Bruce Ismay asks that he be included in the lamentation of those who perished. He feels that he is part of this great expression of grief, that he wants to be part of it too.

Antarctica

(for Richard Ryan)

'I am just going outside and may be some time.'
The others nod, pretending not to know.
At the heart of the ridiculous, the sublime.

He leaves them reading and begins to climb,
Goading his ghost into the howling snow;   5
He is just going outside and may be some time.

The tent recedes beneath its crust of rime
And frostbite is replaced by vertigo:
At the heart of the ridiculous, the sublime.

Need we consider it some sort of crime,   10
This numb self-sacrifice of the weakest? No,
He is just going outside and may be some time —

In fact, for ever. Solitary enzyme,
Though the night yield no glimmer there will glow,
At the heart of the ridiculous, the sublime.   15

He takes leave of the earthly pantomime
Quietly, knowing it is time to go.
'I am just going outside and may be some time.'
At the heart of the ridiculous, the sublime.

Glossary

TITLE Antarctica: the Antarctic is the south polar region; *arktos* in Greek means
'bear', which gives us 'arctic'; 'anti' or 'opposite' and *arktos* gives 'antarctic'.
The great South Pole expedition at the beginning of the twentieth century was
captained by Robert Scott who, together with Edward Wilson, Lawrence Oates, H.
R. Bowers and Edgar Evans, reached the South Pole on 17 January 1912, only to
discover that a Norwegian expedition under Roald Amundsen had beaten them by
a month. None of the five ever made it home. Evans and Oates died first and the
other members of the team perished in late March 1912. Their bodies and diaries
were found by a search party eight months later.
1 'I am just going outside and may be some time': last words recorded by Robert

Scott in his Diary and attributed to Lawrence Oates (1880-1912), who was one of the party of five to reach the South Pole in 1912. On the return journey illness and blizzards caused severe delay. Oates was lamed by frostbite and, convinced that his condition would delay his fellow-explorers' success, walked out into the storm. He deliberately sacrificed his life to help his comrades' chance of survival. On a cairn erected in the Antarctic in November 1912 is the epigraph: 'Hereabouts died a very gallant gentleman, Captain L.E. G. Oates of the Inniskilling Dragoons. In March 1912, returning from the Pole, he walked willingly to his death in a blizzard to try and save his comrades, beset by hardships.' Rory Brennan comments that 'Captain Oates's stiff-upper-lippery in the face of Antarctic starvation is perhaps the best known quote from the first decade of the twentieth century'.

3 sublime: elevated in thought or tone, lofty. 'From the sublime to the ridiculous' is a well-known phrase and is used to describe a movement from one state to an opposite one, where sublime refers to a heightened state, ridiculous to a banal one. Tom Paine in his *Age of Reason* wrote: The sublime and the ridiculous are often so nearly related that it is difficult to class them separately. One step above the sublime makes the ridiculous, and one step above the ridiculous makes the sublime again.'

In 'Antarctica', Mahon shows how Lawrence Oates's apparently ridiculous words and actions achieve a heightened, courageous quality.

5 Goading: urging

7 rime: ice

8 vertigo: dizziness

13 enzyme: the dictionary defines enzyme as 'any one of a large class of protein substances produced by living cells'; here, Mahon uses 'solitary enzyme' as a metaphor for Oates

16 the earthly pantomime: life as a showy spectacle with clowns

The poem is written in the form of a villanelle – a poem of five three-line stanzas and a concluding quatrain. It has the following rhyming scheme: aba aba aba aba aba abaa. 'Antarctica,' according to Derek Mahon, is a feminist poem. Nuala Ni Dhomhnaill says that 'it chronicles the moment when the more-than-faintly-ridiculous heroic male ego snuffs it. The rigidity of the metre and the constant repetitions are a very symptom of the state of the soul. The psyche is an ice-box, a house in mid-winter with the heat turned off. In this state you wander about, metaphorically, in furs and highboots, in a frozen stupor, stamping your feet and repeating yourself constantly. The pipes, the conduits of emotion, are frozen solid, rigid like the lines of the poem. Thus for me 'Antarctica' is the supreme example of a formal poem that is not merely emptily so, but where the metre and strict rhyming scheme play an essential part in building up the reality enacted.'

Questions

1. The glossary offers the background to the poem. What would you consider the poem's central theme?

2. The poem tells of bitter hardship. Examine how this is described. Which words, in your opinion, best capture the Antarctic landscape and the men's mood? How is death viewed in this poem?

3. Why do you think the speaker here thinks that there is 'At the heart of the ridiculous, the sublime'? What is ridiculous? What is sublime?

4. What is the effect of the very regular rhyme scheme and the repetition?

5. Is this a dramatic poem, do you think, or has the poet played down the dramatic qualities?

6. In 'After the Titanic' Derek Mahon portrays Bruce Ismay. Compare and contrast his portrait of Ismay with his portrait of Lawrence Oates in 'Antarctica'. Why are such figures interesting, do you think?

7. This poem has been described as an evocation of 'the cold impenetrable regions of the psyche'. What do you understand by that? Would you agree with this interpretation.

Critical Commentary

This poem begins in the voice of a persona, that of Lawrence Oates, and his one-line utterance is repeated in the final stanza; for the remainder of the poem Mahon re-creates an extraordinary moment in the lives of extraordinary men. In the poems in this selection we have seen how Mahon was drawn to the life of Bruce Ismay and here he is drawn to someone very different. Both poems share very dramatic settings and individuals responding to enormous pressure but Ismay was seen as a coward, Oates as a great hero; one was frightened and selfish, the other courageous and selfless.

The form chosen here, the villanelle, is interesting and, it could be argued, very appropriate. To tell the story of Oates's last moments Mahon has chosen a very ordered, disciplined poetic structure and the repeated rhymes suggest a kind of deliberate numbing quality.

The opening word of the poem are Lawrence Oates's last recorded words and are a striking example of good-manners, diffidence, understatement:

'I am just going outside and may be some time.'
Clearly, Oates felt that he had become a hindrance and had made

a decision to head out into the snow and die. But the words convey nothing self-pitying, histrionic, attention-seeking. And the others on the expedition show the same remarkable restraint. They will honour their companion's decision and grant him the dignity he obviously wants:

> The others nod, pretending not to know

and the first stanza ends with a line which recurs in every second stanza until the final one:

> At the heart of the ridiculous, the sublime.

The first and third line of the opening stanza are woven through the poem and come together to form a concluding couplet. They are, therefore, central to the poem as a whole and sum up the poem's central theme: how heroic sacrifice can be found in what could be viewed as apparently ridiculous words and actions, that there is something magnificent in the 'numb self-sacrifice of the weakest'.

The phrase 'just going outside' does not immediately conjure up the frozen wastes of the Antarctic but that is exactly what the poet creates in stanza two. The tent, it would seem, is cosy, companionable and snug but Oates is willing himself to die in harsh and bitter circumstances:

> He leaves them reading and begins to climb,
> Goading his ghost into the howling snow;
> He is just going outside and may be sometime.

'I am just going outside . . .' has been switched to 'He is just going . . .' and could represent the poet or the men who remain in the tent. There is no suggestion of panic or crisis. Derek Mahon deliberately does not name the men involved and this allows the poem to achieve a greater symbolic power and force. It becomes an image of enforced isolation, an image of breaking away from the group for the welfare of the group, a picture of extraordinary dignity.

The entire poem moves at a measured pace. The lines are slow-moving and suit the slow, determined movement of Oates as he trudges up and on. All hope is being left behind; he is deliberately walking away from it:

> The tent recedes beneath its crust of rime
> And frostbite is replaced by vertigo:
> At the heart of the ridiculous the sublime.

The poem began within the intimate world of the tent and by line five the scene has shifted to the harsh panorama of the white, bitterly cold landscape with its solitary figure.

The speaker's voice becomes more engaged at the beginning of stanza four. The tone is now questioning:

> Need we consider it some sort of crime,
> This numb self-sacrifice of the weakest?

Heroism is being re-defined here. The harsh terms 'crime' and 'weakest' suggest cowardice and shame but the question is answered confidently. The placing of the word 'No' at the end of the line gives the answer greater emphasis:

>   No,
> He is just going outside and may be some time —

but then, in a run-on line, the only one from stanza to stanza in the poem, there is a grim qualification:

>   No,
> He is just going outside and may be some time —
>
> In fact, for ever.

This admission increases our admiration for the solitary figure in the snow. He is determined never to return, never to be a burden. He is a solitary who will radiate light and heat, an image that is singular and all the more striking within the context of the world of the poem:

>   Solitary enzyme
> Though the night yield no glimmer there will glow,
> At the heart of the ridiculous, the sublime.

The final stanza, the only four-line stanza in the villanelle, not only picks up on the two repeated lines but introduces them in a voice that is gentle and supportive. The phrase 'earthly pantomime' gently mocks humanity's endeavours. The speaker attributes to Oates an insight, acceptance and wisdom and his death is seen as a release. The words 'He takes leave' suggests someone in total control and the familiar phrase, 'time to go', here creates a sense of something naturally drawing to a close:

> He takes leave of the earthly pantomime
> Quietly, knowing it is time to go.
> 'I am just going outside and may be some time.'
> At the heart of the ridiculous, the sublime.

The word 'sublime' occurs four times in the poem and so does 'ridiculous', but 'sublime' wins out not only in terms of meaning ('At the heart of the ridiculous the sublime') but sublime is rhymed each time it occurs ('time', 'rime', 'enzyme', 'pantomime'). Even if the speaker does recognise that life may be an 'earthly pantomime' and 'just going outside' is faintly ridiculous, the poem moves towards a strong awareness that Lawrence Oates's act was something noble, grand, majestic.

Sylvia Plath

Sylvia Plath (1932 – 1963)

Sylvia Plath was born on 27 October 1932 in Boston. She was educated at Smith College, Amherst, Massachusetts and at Newnham College, Cambridge where she met and married Ted Hughes in 1956. They taught for a while in America, returned to England and lived in London. Plath's first volume of poems, *The Colossus*, was published in 1960. They moved to Devon in 1961 but the marriage ended and Plath moved back to London with her two young children. There, on 11 February 1963, one of the coldest winters on record, she committed suicide. During the final weeks of her life Plath was writing poem after poem and in 1965, her best known collection, *Ariel* was published. Two other collections were also published posthumously – *Crossing the Water* and *Winter Trees* (both 1971). She also published a novel, *The Bell Jar*. 'The Arrival of the Bee Box' is based on her bee-keeping experiences in Devon; 'Child' was written just two weeks before she died. Plath's life, in her own words, was 'magically run by two electric currents' and these she named 'joyous positive and despairing negative'. Asked once about the importance of poetry Plath said: 'I am not worried that poems reach relatively few people. As it is, they go surprisingly far – among strangers, around the world, even. Farther than the words of a classroom teacher or the prescription of a doctor; if they are very lucky, farther than a lifetime.

Poppies in July (1962)
The Arrival of the Bee Box (1962)
Child (1963)

Poppies in July

[handwritten: Metaphor]

[handwritten: Fires of hell.]

Little poppies, little hell flames,
Do you do no harm? *[handwritten: associated with Devil.]*

You flicker. I cannot touch you.
I put my hands among the flames. Nothing burns.

[handwritten: She wants to have physical pain, to numb her mental pain. (self harm).]

And it exhausts me to watch you *[handwritten: worn out]*   5
Flickering like that, wrinkly and clear red, like the skin of a
mouth.

[handwritten: violent images. (A lot of bloodshed).]
A mouth just bloodied.
Little bloody skirts!

There are fumes that I cannot touch. *[handwritten: A drug produced by them]*
Where are your opiates, your nauseous capsules?   10
[handwritten: The drug lives in the flower,]

If I could bleed, or sleep!——
If my mouth could marry a hurt like that! *[handwritten: Refers to her unhappy marriage..]*

Or your liquors seep to me, in this glass capsule, *[handwritten: Suggests her isolation from the world.]*
Dulling and stilling.
[handwritten: To make her calm.]

But colorless. Colorless.   15

[handwritten: May refere to the opiate, or may or a. Trance like state the poet wants to enter]

20 July 1962

Glossary

Title: Poppies – cornfield flowers usually red but also white and yellow; opium poppy associated with drug-induced sleep – opium is extracted from white poppy seeds

10 opiates: drugs, narcotics
10 nauseous: sickening
10 capsules: little gelatine containers holding medicine
13 glass capsule: a bell jar?
14 dulling and stilling: Anne Stevenson comments that when Plath was depressed 'there was a turning in on herself, a longing for nonbeing, "dulling and stilling" as in "Poppies in July."' This is one of only three poems Plath wrote in July 1962 (the others are 'The Other' and 'Words heard, by accident, over the phone'); all are directed at Assia Wevill, with whom Ted Hughes was having an affair. 'Poppies in July' is the least explicit. In Ronald Hayman's words 'Assia's presence can be felt only indirectly, but it seems to be contributing to the appearance of the poppies, which are like little hell flames, wrinkly and clear red, or like the skin of a bloodied mouth.'

Questions

1. The title indicates that this is a poem about flowers in summer. Is it what one would expect of a poem on such a topic? When does the reader first realise that it is not a typical poem?

2. How would you describe the mind of the speaker in this poem? Which details support your opinion? What is the effect of the exclamation marks?

3. How are the poppies described by the speaker? List the different images and whether you think that there is a connection or similarity among them?

4. Does the speaker's mood change as you read through the poem? How would you describe the mood in the closing line?

Critical Commentary

The title announces summer flowers, but by the end of the poem's first line the flowers have acquired a dangerous and sinister quality. The speaker sees them as 'little hell flames'. The poppies are untouchable; if the poet puts her hands among the flowers they have no effect:

Little poppies, little hell flames,
Do you do no harm?

You flicker. I cannot touch you.
I put my hands among the flames. Nothing burns.

The repeated 'little' in the opening line suggests tenderness but 'hell flames' alters the image and creates a sense of evil. Putting her hands among the flames suggests a impulse for self-inflicted suffering but 'Nothing burns'.

The poppies are exhausting and unattractive. Other images follow, unusual or unattractive or both:

And it exhausts me to watch you
Flickering like that, wrinkly and clear red, like the skin
of a mouth.

A mouth just bloodied.
Little bloody skirts!

All description is subjective and the way Plath sees these poppies in July reveals something of Plath's frame of mind. Why should these poppies be unattractive, dangerous and fascinating to her? She does not tell the reader. The link made in the poem between the wrinkly, clear red poppies and an injured mouth presents the reader with the presence or the possibility of physical violence.

There is a shift in focus from line nine. The poppies are no longer before us but the speaker wishes for the drugged state the poppy is associated with. Violence or sleep are seen as preferred states to her present one. The speaker longs for escape and the opiates of the poppies are seen as a means of releasing her into a numbed, inert state where everything would be 'colorless. Colorless'.

In the opening stanzas the poppies are alive and colourful, flame red and bloody and flickering, but their constant movement and colour are rejected for a world drained of colour and inert. The poem moves quietly towards a death-wish. Plath writes that the opiates are 'nauseous'; she is not blind to the sickening quality of the drug and yet she chooses it, which suggests her determination and desperation.

The question marks and the exclamation marks indicate a fascination (line two), a feeling of repulsion (line eight), a desperation (line ten) and an intense longing (lines eleven and twelve).

The Arrival of the Bee Box Confinment.

I ordered this, this clean wood box
Square as a chair and almost too heavy to lift.
I would say it was the coffin of a midget
Or a square baby *Disturbing association with death.*
Were there not such a din in it. *Loud noise*   5

The box is locked, it is dangerous. *Sense of Dred*
I have to live with it overnight
And I can't keep away from it.
There are no windows, so I can't see what is in there.
There is only a little grid, no exit.   10

Ambivalent attitude to box/ Fascinated/ Excited

I put my eye to the grid.
It is dark, dark,
With the swarmy feeling of African hands *Claustrophobic*
Minute and shrunk for export,
Black on black, angrily clambering. *She moves closer*   15
to the box.

How can I let them out?
It is the noise that appalls me most of all,
The unintelligible syllables. *incoherent.*
It is like a Roman mob,
Small, taken one by one, but my god, together!   20

I lay my ear to furious Latin.
I am not a Caesar.
I have simply ordered a box of maniacs.
They can be sent back.
They can die, I need feed them nothing, I am the owner.   25

I wonder how hungry they are.
I wonder if they would forget me
If I just undid the locks and stood back and turned into a tree.
There is the laburnum, its blond colonnades,
And the petticoats of the cherry.   30

They might ignore me immediately
In my moon suit and funeral veil.
I am no source of honey
So why should they turn on me?
Tomorrow I will be sweet God, I will set them free.   35

The box is only temporary.

Glossary

10 grid: wire network
13 swarmy: swarm-like – as in a large, dense group
22 Caesar: Roman ruler
29 colonnades: long column-like flowering branches
32 moon suit: the boiler-suit, worn by Plath as protection when tending bees, is like that worn by an astronaut

Questions

1. Would you consider this a memorable poem? Give reasons for your answer, supporting the points you make by quoting from the text.

2. How would you describe the speaker's reaction to the bee box. Fascination? Unease? Fear? Look at each stanza in turn. How does she portray herself?

3. Discuss how Plath creates a dramatic atmosphere in 'The Arrival of the Bee Box'. Which words and phrases are particularly effective?

4. What has this poem to say about power and control? Consider the significance of 'Caesar' and 'sweet God'.

5. In this thirty-six line poem the speaks uses 'I' eighteen times. Consider the 'I' phrases in sequence. Read them aloud. What is the effect of the poet's use of 'I' here?

6. Choose three interesting images and say why you found them so.

7. Is the subject matter of bees in a bee box something which you would associate with Plath? Compare and contrast this poem with other poems by Plath which focus on nature – 'Black Rook in Rainy Weather', 'Pheasant', 'Elm', 'Poppies in July'. Is Sylvia Plath a typical nature poet?

8. Comment on the way the poem is shaped on the page. In your answer you should consider Plath's use of the long and short line, her use of repetition, the stanza divisions and the final, separate line.

9. Of this poem Nuala Ní Dhomhnaill says: 'The poem fairly buzzes with energy, not the least of which is the energy of simple, colloquial words and phrases – "coffin of a midget," "a square baby," "I have simply ordered a box of maniacs," yet the whole is greater than its parts.' What, in your opinion, is the 'whole' of the poem?

10. Compare and contrast Elizabeth Bishop's poem 'The Fish' and Sylvia Plath's poem 'The Arrival of the Bee Box' as poems which explore the significance of power and control.

Critical Commentary

The subject matter or the little drama of this poem is straightforward: 'I have ordered a box of bees for a beehive in the garden'. What is remarkable and interesting about this poem, like so many of Sylvia Plath's poems, is her response and reaction to the box of bees when it is delivered. There is no other person mentioned in the poem and the experience of viewing the swarm of bees is fascinating, compulsive, intense.

The poem begins in a matter-of-fact way:

> I ordered this, this clean wood box

but Plath's individual and unusual way of viewing things can be seen in the imagery, a mixture of domestic and eerily strange. This clean wood box is

> Square as a chair and almost too heavy to lift.
> I would say it was the coffin of a midget
> Or a square baby
> Were there not such a din in it.

The 'coffin', 'midget', 'square baby' all suggest the negative, the abnormal. The bee box, within three lines, has become something strange and sinister. The first stanza works on the eye and the ear: lines 2-4 give us the shape, line five, with its onomatopoeic 'din in it', gives us the sound.

Though the box is locked it is dangerous and most of the poem records Plath's total fascination with the trapped bees: 'I can't keep away from it'. There is no escape, but the speaker describes how she is drawn to the world of the bees within the box. The language is stark, straightforward, as in:

> There are no windows, so I can't see what is in there

but then, in a series of powerful images, the bees become imprisoned, badly treated Africans and a Roman mob. Her thinking about them as black slaves prompts her to free them ('How can I let them out?'):

> I put my eye to the grid.
> It is dark, dark,
> With the swarmy feeling of African hands
> Minute and shrunk for export,
> Black on black, angrily clambering.

The repetition in 'dark, dark' and 'Black on black', the sensuous details of 'swarmy' and 'shrunk', the energy of 'angrily clambering' create a hidden, claustrophobic scene of heat, dark oppression and helpless desperation.

With the question 'How can I let them out?' comes a different tone. There was a distancing in the opening lines; gradually the speaker is more and more involved.

The noise terrifies her and the image of the bees as an unruly Roman mob suggests chaos, danger. She saw them as Africans; she hears them as Romans:

> I lay my ear to furious Latin.
> I am not a Caesar.
> I have simply ordered a box of maniacs.

It is then that she reconsiders her role. Though she viewed them as frighteningly noisy, she now views herself as all powerful, determining:

> They can be sent back.
> They can die, I need feed them nothing, I am the
> owner.

With these statements she imagines herself playing at Caesar. She is in total control. The bees are entirely dependent on her and a more caring note is introduced:

> I wonder how hungry they are.
> I wonder if they would forget me
> If I just undid the locks and stood back and turned
> into a tree.
> There is the laburnum, its blond colonnades,
> And the petticoats of the cherry.

There is also a wonderful sense of the bees in their element – not unnaturally locked in a square box – but free to visit the glorious and lyrical laburnum and cherry trees. The contrast between the confined, crowded world of the box and the freedom that is possible causes the speaker to dwell on how it is possible for her to play 'sweet God'. She is 'not a Caesar' and therefore incapable of controlling a Roman mob but she is empowered and capable of releasing the bee prisoners: tomorrow 'I will set them free'.

Here the speaker is active, not passive. The speaker's presence is felt throughout: ten sentences begin with 'I' and 'I' is used eighteen times in all. She in control, not a victim, and the furious, frantic energy of the bees will end because of her. The poem explores the possibility of power and control and the poem concludes: 'The box is only temporary'.

Sylvia Plath's father, a distinguished entomologist, who died when she was eight, had written a standard work on bees: Bumblebees and Their Ways. Even the subject matter of a poem such as 'The Arrival of the Bee Box' would have special significance and resonance for Otto Plath's daughter.

Child

[handwritten: Everything else is TARNISHED.]

Your clear eye is the one absolutely beautiful thing. *[handwritten underline: the one]*
I want to fill it with color and ducks, *[handwritten: EXCIMENT.]*
The zoo of the new *[handwritten: INNOCENTS]*

Whose names you meditate— *[handwritten: REFLECT UPON.]*
April snowdrop, Indian pipe, *[handwritten: WHITE]* *[handwritten: A WOODLAND FLOWER.]*   5
Little

Stalk without wrinkle, *[handwritten: EQUALS THE CHILD.]*
Pool in which images
Should be grand and classical *[handwritten: METAPHOR / For the Child to see things.]*

Not this troublous   10
Wringing of hands, this dark *[handwritten left margin: WRINGING OF HANDS]*
Ceiling without a star. *[handwritten: THIS DARK Ceiling of HER MIND.]*

[handwritten: CLASIC IMAGE OF DISPARE]

28 January 1963

Glossary

5 Indian pipe: leafless American plant with single flower resembling a tobacco pipe
6/7 Little/Stalk: small stem of plant
9 classical: beautiful, noble
10 troublous: full of troubles, disturbed

Ronald Hayman, in The Death and Life of Sylvia Plath, sums up this poem as follows: '[Plath's] frustrated yearning for domestic happiness is tenderly expressed in 'Child', which juxtaposes darkness and lamentation with beautiful young eyes which ought to be feasted on colours and ducks.'

Sylvia Plath's son, Nicholas was born on 17 January 1962.
This poem, dated 28 January 1963, was written just two weeks before Plath died on 11 February 1963.

Questions

1. How would you describe the speaker's tone in the poem's opening line? Why do you think it is the longest line in the poem?

2. The American essayist and poet Henry David Thoreau said that 'every child begins the world again'. Do you think the speaker here conveys a similar idea? Give reasons for your answer.

3. There is a clear difference between the world of the child and the speaker's world. Which words best capture that difference, in your opinion?

4. What mood is created by the images in the poem's final stanza? Do you think this an optimistic or a pessimistic poem?

5. What effect did this poem have on you? Of the poems by Plath on your course which one did you like best? Admire the most?

Critical Commentary

It is difficult not to read Sylvia Plath's poems in the light of her life and death. Knowing that she wrote 'Child' on 28 January 1963 and that she died, two weeks later, by her own hand on 11 February 1963 at the age of thirty, the poem becomes charged with a heartbreaking sadness. It is one of the last things Plath wrote [she wrote eight other poems after 'Child'] and one of the most poignant. It celebrates her child; it expresses her love for her child and it tells of her own disturbed, troubled state.

The poem begins with an image of beauty, health, happiness. The tone is immediate and involved. The longest line in the poem, the opening line, is a line expressing total joy. There is a longing to give:

> Your clear eye is the one absolutely beautiful thing.
> I want to fill it with color and ducks,
> The zoo of the new

The poem becomes a collection of nursery toys, beautiful things, most of its one sentence offering a sense of the child's potential, its life ahead. 'The zoo of the new' is effective in summoning up a sense of delight and excitement, just like the delight and excitement in a young child on visiting a zoo. This is what should be, the poet is saying; this is what she wants: delights and wonders, those things that will bring happiness.

> Whose names you meditate—
> April snowdrop, Indian pipe

Life's fragile beauty is contained in the image of the snowdrop; the image of the 'Little/ Stalk without wrinkle' suggests newness, freshness. The mother sees her child as a pool:

> Pool in which images
> Should be grand and classical

The poem so far paints a hopeful picture of child and childhood but the poem ends with a dark and agitated reflection in the pool of childhood. It is how Plath sees herself, projecting her anxieties and sorrows on to the child. The child should only see things that are noble and dignified:

> Not this troublous
> Wringing of hands, this dark
> Ceiling without a star.

In contrast with the life-enhancing words and images in the earlier part of the poem, these final words are negative and grim. The speaker undoubtedly loves her child but seems helpless and unable to protect it from harm.

Adrienne Rich

Adrienne Rich (b. 1929)

Poet and political activist, Adrienne [pronounced AHdrienne] Rich was born 'white and middle-class' on 16 May 1929 in Baltimore, Maryland. Her father encouraged her to write: 'I tried for a long time to please him, or rather, not to displease him'. Her grandmother and mother, Rich said, were 'frustrated artists and intellectuals, a lost writer and a lost composer between them.' In 1951 she graduated from Radcliffe College, part of Harvard University, in Cambridge, Massachusetts. Her first collection, *A Change of World*, was chosen by W.H. Auden for the Yale Younger Poets Award. In 1953 she married a Harvard economist, had three sons, lived in Cambridge Mass. and moved to New York in 1966. Rich left her husband in 1970 and he died that same year. Over the last forty years Adrienne Rich has published more than sixteen volumes of poetry, four books of non-fiction prose and has won numerous awards. She writes of being white, Jewish, radical and lesbian in America; she writes 'in full knowledge that the majority of the world's illiterates are woman, that I live in a technologically advanced country where 40% of the people can barely read and 20% are functionally illiterate.' Themes central to Rich's work include power, gender, sexuality, the private, the political. 'Aunt Jennifer's Tigers' explores male power and authority within a domestic setting; 'Storm Warnings' looks at change and its implications; 'Power' celebrates an extraordinary selfless woman, Marie Curie, who dedicated herself to scientific knowledge and discovery and did so with courage and determination. Adrienne Rich has lived in California since 1984 where she taught English and feminist studies at Stanford University until 1992.

Aunt Jennifer's Tigers
The Uncle Speaks in the Drawing Room

Aunt Jennifer's Tigers

Aunt Jennifer's tigers prance across a screen,
Bright topaz denizens of a world of green.
They do not fear the men beneath the tree;
They pace in sleek chivalric certainty.

Aunt Jennifer's fingers fluttering through her wool   5
Find even the ivory needle hard to pull.
The massive weight of Uncle's wedding band
Sits heavily upon Aunt Jennifer's hand.

When Aunt is dead, her terrified hands will lie
Still ringed with ordeals she was mastered by.   10
The tigers in the panel that she made
Will go on prancing, proud and unafraid.

Glossary

1 prance: bound, spring forward from hind legs
1 screen: an ornamental panel placed before an empty firegrate or used to keep off the heat from a fire. Not very common nowadays.
2 topaz: the golden, yellow colour of the precious stone
2 denizens: inhabitants
4 sleek: smooth, glossy
4 chivalric: brave, gallant, like knights
6 ivory: made of animal tusk
10 ordeals: difficult experiences, severe trials, endurances

Rich, in her essay 'When We Dead Awaken' (1971), says: "Looking back at poems I wrote before I was twenty-one, I'm startled because beneath the conscious craft are glimpses of the split I even then experienced between the girl who wrote poems, who defined herself writing poems, and the girl who was to define herself by her relationships with men. 'Aunt Jennifer's Tigers' (1951), written while I was a student, looks with deliberate detachment at this split."

Questions

1. Having read through the text how would you act out this poem? How could a class group create an effective tableau of the situation within the poem?

2. Draw your version of the panel or screen that Aunt Jennifer is embroidering. What does the image tell us about the relationship between men and animals?

3. The poem is a series of descriptions, statements, imaginings. Which of these is the most powerful in your opinion?

4. Comment on 'fluttering' and 'massive'.

5. What does the regular rhyme contribute to the overall effective? Does the poem's formal structure match its theme? Explain.

6. What is the effect of the rhythm and rhyme here?

7. Is this, in your opinion, an out-of-date poem for today's teenage reader? Give reasons for your answer.

8. Why do you think that Adrienne Rich ends her poem with a reference to the tigers 'prancing, proud and unafraid'?

Critical Commentary

Rich was twenty-one when this poem was published in her first collection, A Change of World. On the page, this poem looks neat, formal and well-organised. There are three four-line stanzas, several of the lines are written in iambic pentameter and there is a regular end-rhyme (aabb, ccdd, eeff). The poem may seem conventional but there is a feminist quality to the poem which makes it powerful and memorable and prompts important questions about gender issues. 'Aunt Jennifer's Tigers' focuses on a familiar theme, that of marriage, in this instance the speaker's aunt and uncle but the relationship at the heart of the poem is unequal. The woman, Aunt Jennifer, is oppressed by her dominating husband. Though the aunt and uncle are fictional this does not diminish the power or the impact of the poem.

The title suggests something powerful, exotic, unusual. The tigers in this instance belong to an embroidered image which Aunt Jennifer is working on. Aunt Jennifer's choice of image, in this context, is interesting. She is creating strong, fearless, untamed creatures the very opposite of her own life.

The poem's opening lines are powerful and are filled with movement and colour. Everything would suggest confidence, energy. The verbs 'prance' and 'pace' with the alliterative echo, the colours "topaz' and 'green' create an upbeat feeling. That these wild animals do not fear 'men' adds to their powerful presence. The use of 'Bright' brings the embroidered panel alive. Aunt Jennifer has created these creatures; it is a striking creative act.

In the second stanza the mood changes. The energy ebbs. The speaker tells us that Aunt Jennifer's fingers are 'fluttering through her wool' which suggests nervousness, unease. The making of the panel, vividly described in stanza one, is difficult and the poet speaks of the 'massive weight of Uncle's wedding band'. The wife is engaged in making a decorative, embroidered panel but her husband's presence, their marriage, 'Sits heavily' upon Aunt Jennifer. The never-ending circle of the wedding ring usually symbolizes eternity, union but in this instance the speaker sees it as a massive, heavy presence. Aunt Jennifer is trapped in a marriage and it is as if the tapestry she weaves is her only means of speaking.

The poem begins in the present tense but in the final stanza the poet focuses on the future. Here the speaker imagines a time when Aunt Jennifer is dead. The words 'terrified', 'ordeals', 'mastered' capture the attitude of the niece as she contemplates her aunt's life. The image of the wedding ring recurs in the image of the aunt's life 'ringed with ordeals'. It's an unattractive portrait of a marriage – the husband is controlling. Even in death Aunt Jennifer is terrified. And yet the poem's final image is one of freedom, escape, fearlessness. The brave, gallant tigers 'Will go on prancing, proud and unafraid'. The final two lines, perfect iambic pentameters, are charged with energy and convey a feeling of defiance. Aunt Jennifer, though she was cowed into submission, succeeded in creating an image of assertion. The hands that fluttered and found 'even the ivory needle hard to pull' paradoxically made possible the very opposite: an image of certain power and pride.

The poem offers a glimpse of Aunt Jennifer's life. The speaker expresses an opinion but does not pass judgement. It could be argues that the male/female divide is depicted in a simplistic manner: the man is a bully; the woman is a victim and yet it prompts important questions about the nature of relationships, marriage, self-assertion and creativity. 'Aunt Jennifer's Tigers' is also a very fine illustration of the power of symbol.

The Uncle Speaks in the Drawing Room

(Posh house) — handwritten

Not told who's uncle — handwritten margin

I have seen the mob of late — *Group of people*
Standing sullen in the square,
Gazing with a sullen stare — *angry*
At window, balcony, and gate.
Some have talked in bitter tones,   5
Some have held and fingered stones. — *Held ready to throw.*

These are follies that subside.
Let us consider, none the less,
Certain frailties of glass
Which, it cannot be denied,   10
Lead in times like these to fear — *Social unrest is implied*
For crystal vase and chandelier. — *"in time's like these".*
upper class world.
Not that missiles will be cast;
None as yet dare lift an arm. — *Not for sure.*
But the scene recalls a storm — *GRANDAD*   15
When our grandsire stood aghast — *shock.*
To see his antique ruby bowl
Shivered in a thunder-roll.

Let us only bear in mind
How these treasures handed down   20
From a calmer age passed on
Are in the keeping of our kind.
We stand between the dead glass-blowers
And murmurings of missile-throwers.

Margin notes (left):
Repetition of sullen
Highlights Resentment
Uncle referred his valuable goods
Scare to break
Still focusing on material goods.
it implys that the glass blowers were of more cultured

Glossary

TITLE: Drawing Room – an elegant and beautifully furnished room; originally
'withdrawing-room' – a room to which the company withdraws after dinner; also
the room to which ladies withdraw from the dining-room after dinner
1 mob: the rabble, the vulgar, the common people; a disorderly crowd, a riotous
assembly [from Latin mobile vulgus = excitable/mobile crowd]
2 sullen: angry, silent
7 follies: foolish behaviour
13 missiles: weapons/objects that can be thrown or fired
16 grandsire: grandsire is an old-fashioned word for grandfather (sire means a
senior or elder)
16 aghast: terrified, frightened
22 in the keeping of our kind: in the custody and safe-keeping of people like us

169

Questions

1. What is the effect of 'The Uncle' as opposed to 'Uncle' or 'My Uncle' in the title? Comment on 'Speaks' as opposed to, say, 'shouts'. What do the words 'Drawing Room' suggest?

2. The poet here is speaking in the voice of The Uncle. Which words in stanza one best sum up the mob in the square? What image do the words 'window, balcony, and gate summon up'?

3. Consider the effect of the drumbeat rhyme and rhythm in the opening lines. How do they suit what is being said?

4. The Uncle is confident ('These are follies that subside' – line 7) that the mob is not a realistic or serious threat. Who is he addressing when he says 'Let us consider'? What, do you think, has created that confidence?

5. He fears for 'crystal vase and chandelier'. What do these precious objects symbolise?

6. How would you describe the Uncle's tone? Smug? Superior? How do you respond to line 22: 'the keeping of our kind'?

7. What does this poem say about the relationship between the privileged classes and the ordinary people?

8. Does this read like a poem from the 1950s? Why? Why not?

9. What does this poem say about the past, the present, the future? What does this poem say about women?

10. This poem was written by an American woman in the world's supposedly greatest democracy. Why do you think Adrienne Rich wrote such a poem? Does it make you angry? Does it sadden you? Do you think it a political poem? Give reasons for your answers.

Critical Commentary

Rich here uses a male persona and like 'Storm Warnings' the poem speaks of unrest, threat. In this instance, however, the disturbance is explicitly political. It refers to people power and their disquiet. That the title refers to uncle as 'The Uncle' not 'My Uncle' or 'An Uncle' gives the poem a particular tone. The setting of 'the Drawing Room' also creates an atmosphere of order, elegance, privilege. There is an interior world and an outer world. The aunt and uncle in 'Aunt Jennifer's Tigers' were not real people; the same may be true of this particular uncle but he stands for a way of viewing the world that is strikingly memorable.

One of the most notable aspects of this poem is picked up by the ear on a first reading. The regular rhyme scheme [abbacc] and the seven-syllable line used throughout establishes an authoritative and confident tone of voice. The speaker is a commanding presence. He speaks from his drawing room in a house with 'balcony, and gate' which suggests an impressive, wealthy structure.

The people outside the gate are referred to by the Uncle as 'the mob'. They are a 'sullen' presence and their discontent and silent anger are associated with their 'gazing' at this house. We are never told much about the Uncle's life or profession. He is wealthy and he has inherited wealth but if he is political or not we are never told. But this is a poem that is preoccupied with politics. It looks at privilege, inheritance, inequality but all from the Uncle's perspective.

The opening stanza contains an atmosphere of menace. The reader hears in the Uncle's voice a tone of distaste. The word 'mob' and the repeated use of 'sullen' ['I have seen the mob of late/ Standing sullen in the square./ Gazing with a sullen stare'] convey a superior attitude. The closing two lines in stanza one summon up an image of a disgruntled group. There is nothing to suggest that these people are not justified in their protest.

Stanza two refers to these people's actions as 'follies'. The uncle is not too troubled by these people beyond the gate; he feels that their sullen presence will fade away. To refer to their behaviour as foolish ['follies'] is unsympathetic, patronizing, condescending. Lines 8-12 ['Let us consider . . . chandelier'] are preoccupied with the speaker's concerns for his opulent possessions. The contrast between the world of the gated house and the public square is sharpened by such details as 'fingered stones' and 'crystal vase and chandelier'.

The third stanza begins with a smug tone. The Uncle is confident that no missiles will be thrown and yet he offers an historical perspective when an earlier 'storm' resulted in an ancestor's 'antique ruby bowl' being 'Shivered in a thunder-roll'. That upheaval is spoken of in terms of a storm but it could also perhaps refer to a political riot or upheaval?

The irony here is very effective. The Uncle speaks as if the reader will agree with his view of things. He presumes that he is speaking to like-minded people. The use of 'us' [line 19] and 'We' [line 23] would suggest this. The Uncle's main concern is his material wealth and possessions. The earlier age is viewed as 'calmer' but he feels that it is his duty to ensure that the divide between privileged and underprivileged be maintained. The poem's final line is an interesting image of the world since c. 1950 when this poem was written. The Uncle does not welcome change. It suits him to be conservative.

William Shakespeare

William Shakespeare
(1564 – 1616)

Though more books have been written about Shakespeare than
any other writer, very little is known about his life. He was born
in Stratford-upon-Avon and the birth date is thought to be 23
April, which is also the date of his death. Records show that
Shakespeare was baptised on 26 April 1564, the eldest son of
John Shakespeare and Mary Arden and one of eight children,
three of whom did not survive childhood. At eighteen, William
Shakespeare married twenty-six year old Anne Hathaway,
and they had three children, Susanna and twins Hamnet and
Judith. Both daughters outlived their father, but Hamnet died
when he was eleven. Shakespeare, as a young man, moved to
London on his own, where he acted and wrote. In addition to
the sequence of 154 sonnets, not written for publication, he
also wrote narrative poems and thirty-seven plays. He retired
to Stratford, where he died in 1616. He is buried there in Holy
Trinity Church.

'Shall I compare thee to a summer's day?' (18)
'Like as the waves make towards the pebbled shore' (60)

Sonnet 18

Shall I compare thee to a summer's day?
Thou art more lovely and more temperate.
Rough winds do shake the darling buds of May,
And summer's lease hath all too short a date.
Sometime too hot the eye of heaven shines,   5
And often is his gold complexion dimmed;
And every fair from fair sometime declines,
By chance, or nature's changing course, untrimmed;
But thy eternal summer shall not fade,
Nor lose possession of that fair thou ow'st,   10
Nor shall Death brag thou wander'st in his shade,
When in eternal lines to time thou grow'st.
  So long as men can breathe or eyes can see,
  So long lives this, and this gives life to thee.

Glossary

1 summer's day: 'as good as one shall see on a summer's day' meaning 'as good as it gets' is a proverbial phrase
2 temperate: of a mild temperature / equable / not susceptible to extremes
3 May: in the 1590s the English calendar was different – Shakespeare's May was part of what we now know as June. May was summer then.
4 lease: the time allotted to summer [lease and possession, line 10, are legal terms] hath all too short a date: has too short a duration
5 Sometime: sometimes
5 the eye of heaven: here the sun imagery from Sonnet 7 recurs
7 fair from fair: beautiful thing from its beautiful state
7 sometime: eventually, at some time
8 untrimmed: stripped of ornament
10 ow'st: have / possess
11 Nor shall. . . shade: – cf. Psalms 23,3: 'Yea, though I walk through the valley of the shadow of death, I will fear no evil: for thou art with me, thy rod and thy staff be the things that do comfort me.'
12 eternal lines: the poet's immortal lines or the lines of life, lineage.

Questions

1. In the opening line Shakespeare asks a question. A summer's day in this instance means as good as the best there is, the pinnacle of perfection. Do you think he has found other comparisons and rejected those before rejecting the image of 'a summer's day'? Why?

2. What reasons are given for rejecting the comparison of the loved one to a summer's day? What is the effect of this?

3. What is signalled by the word 'But' at the beginning of the third quatrain? What is the effect of 'Nor' and its repetition? How does the poet make clear his argument in lines 9 to 14? What makes his argument convincing? In your answer you should consider details such as 'summer's lease' (line 4) and 'eternal summer' (line 9).

4. Much of the sonnet is preoccupied with transience and immortality. How does Sonnet 18 compare with Sonnet 12 under these two headings?

What difference is there in the concluding couplets?

5. The poem's logical argument contains the particular and the general. Why does one give way to the other? What is the effect of this? Why does Shakespeare use both?

Critical Commentary

Sonnets 1 - 17 in the 154 Sonnet Sequence urge procreation. In Sonnet 18 the young man achieves immortality through the very poem which celebrates him. [Most likely you will have heard in relation to Shakespeare's Sonnets various theories as to the identity of the young man (sonnets 1 - 126) and the Dark Lady (sonnets 127 - 152), who are addressed in the sequence. Some cite these sonnets to a young man as evidence of Shakespeare's homosexuality, but 'lover', for example, in Shakespeare's day was the same as 'friend'. People signed their letters 'Thy lover' or 'Your ever true lover', and such phrases were, in Stephen Booth's words, 'as neutral sexually as the salutation "Dear Sir"'. However, 'lover' could also mean more than friend, depending on the context, and there have been endless discussions of Shakespeare's sexuality, all to no avail. The final word I think should be given to Stephen Booth who writes: 'HOMOSEXUALITY: William Shakespeare was almost certainly homosexual, bisexual, or heterosexual. The sonnets provide no evidence on the matter.']

This sonnet is also addressed to a young man, but his immortality is now found, not in his children, but in the very poem itself which praises him. Sonnet 18 begins with a question in line 1:

> Shall I compare thee to a summer's day?

and it is answered in the subsequent lines of the sonnet. A summer's day is mentioned here as the ultimate loveliness, but Shakespeare debunks the conventional view. A summer's day is not lovely enough a comparison

> Thou art more lovely and more temperate.

Here an intimacy is achieved by the use of 'I' and 'thou', and the placing of both 'Shall I' and 'Thou art' at the beginning of lines 1 and 2

> Shall **I** compare thee to a summer's day?
> **Thou** art more lovely and more temperate

gives the 'I' and the 'thou' greater emphasis.

Line 2 is a very definite rejection of the image in line 1. Shakespeare's use of 'more' and its repetition emphasises his feelings, and the lines which follow strengthen his argument. He presents example upon example, reason after reason why a summer's day is not an apt image for this young man:

> Rough winds do shake the darling buds of May,
> And summer's lease hath all too short a date;

A summer's day can be uncomfortable; summer itself is short-lived. Lines 3-6 is a catalogue of shortcomings; Shakespeare's use of 'And' at the beginning of lines 4, 6 and 7 indicates yet another reason why the summer's day image is inadequate and it strengthens his argument:

> And summer's lease hath all too short a date;
> Sometime too hot the eye of heaven shines,
> And often is his gold complexion dimmed;
> And every fair from fair sometime declines,
> By chance or nature's changing course untrimmed

The vocabulary here is preoccupied with change and flux, the unreliable and the inevitable: 'too short', 'Sometime', 'often', 'dimmed', 'sometime declines', 'chance', 'changing', 'untrimmed'. A summer's day can be 'too short' or 'too hot' and, even when it is beautiful, its beauty is transient.

Having focused on the particular, one summer's day, Shakespeare then moves from the particular to the general. By line 7 he speaks of how 'every fair' or beautiful thing 'sometime declines'. Just like the summer day does, they too must come to an end. The reader's own experience will confirm that what Shakespeare is saying is true. Many beautiful things do not last forever and of course our knowing this is another reason for the success of the argument.

Up until now (the first two quatrains), Shakespeare has been dismissing a conventional image of perfection as inadequate. In a confidently dismissive tone he clearly argued why he shall not compare this young man to a summer's day. Line 9 has a new and justified confidence. A summer's day will come to an end and therefore is an inadequate image, but Shakespeare has discovered a means of conferring immortality upon his friend:

> But thy eternal summer shall not fade,
> Nor lose possession of that fair thou ow'st,
> Nor shall death brag thou wand'rest in his shade,
> When in eternal lines to time thou grow'st.

'But' marks a new found tone, a tone of conviction, and the series of phrases which express this belief,

> . . . . shall not fade,
> Nor lose possession . . . .
> Nor shall death brag . . . . . .

add to the argument line by line.

And the final line in the third quatrain

> When in eternal lines to time thou grow'st

is separate from and different from the passing of time as portrayed in the first eleven lines of the sonnet.

The word 'eternal' in line 12 is a crucial contrast; all mention of time up to now has been concerned with its transient nature. Now the passing of time will make possible growth, not decline. The 'eternal lines' of the poem will live, as Shakespeare tells us in the couplet,

> So long as men can breathe or eyes can see,

and the concluding line with its repetitions and absolute confidence give the sonnet, which was so preoccupied with things passing, a double immortality, the immortality of the loved one and the immortality of the poem itself:

> So long lives this, and this gives life to thee.

Every word in the couplet is monosyllabic and the iambic pentameter meter (a five foot line consisting of five iambs, an iamb being an unstressed syllable, followed by a stressed syllable), if exaggerated, would sound like this:

> So **long** as **men** can **breathe** or **eyes** can **see**,
> So **long** lives **this**, and **this** gives **life** to **thee**.

Obviously no one should read the poem in this exaggerated manner, but to understand where the emphases fall is to understand more clearly how the poem communicates its central ideas. But the monosyllabic words and the stress pattern together give the concluding couplet great power and force.
In 1976 Howard Moss wrote the following:

> Shall I Compare Thee to a Summer's Day?
>
> Who says you're like one of the dog days?
> You're nicer. And better.
> Even in May, the weather can be gray,
> And a summer sub-let doesn't last forever.
> Sometimes the sun's too hot;
> Sometimes it is not.
> Who can stay young forever?
> People break their necks or just drop dead!
> But you? Never!
> If there's just one condensed reader left
> Who can figure out the abridged alphabet,
> > After you're dead and gone,
> > In this poem you'll live on.

Howard Moss set out to say the same thing as Shakespeare says in Sonnet 18, but the differences between Moss and Shakespeare, especially in terms of technique, highlight the individual aspects of each poem. [Here is a good moment to stop and ask yourself if a poem is better because it is understood immediately.]

Sonnet 18 has moved from the brightness of a summer's day in its opening line and 'the eye of heaven' which 'shines' in line 5 through 'dimmed', 'declines', 'fade', until it speaks of 'shade' in line 11. The phrase 'gives life' in the final line is set against the inevitable decline of the summer's day and the decline of all things fair; the particular attention given to 'this . . . this' in line 14 brings the reader even closer to the very words on the page and the poem itself, for in the very act of reading we are proving Shakespeare's idea true. He is conscious of the making of the poem and the act of reading the poem; it is our breathing and our eyes which make possible the experience, and this knowing awareness invites us and involves us more closely with the poem.

Sonnet 60

Like as the waves make towards the pebbled shore,
So do our minutes hasten to their end;
Each changing place with that which goes before,
In sequent toil all forwards do contend.
Nativity, once in the main of light,   5
Crawls to maturity, wherewith being crown'd,
Crooked eclipses 'gainst his glory fight,
And Time that gave doth now his gift confound.
Time doth transfix the flourish set on youth,
And delves the parallels in beauty's brow,   10
Feeds on the rarities of nature's truth,
And nothing stands but for his scythe to mow.
    And yet to times in hope my verse shall stand,
    Praising thy worth, despite his cruel hand.

Glossary

3 It has been pointed out that this line is inaccurate – waves do not change places
with one another. It has also been pointed out that as each wave ebbs from the
beach it does appear to slide under the next, incoming wave.
4 In sequent toil: through successive efforts
4 contend: strive
5 Nativity: the new-born child
5 once: no sooner
5 main of light: the whole of light / the world of light / the open sea of light – after
the darkness of the womb.
6 wherewith: with which
7 Crooked: malignant.
8 his gift: the growth to maturity.
8 confound: destroy / ruin.
9 transfix: destroy / remove / pierce through.
10 delves: digs.
11 rarities: the most excellent things.
13 times in hope: future time only dreamed of.

Questions

1. This sonnet also tells of the inexorable passing of time and praises the un-named young man. Why do you think that Shakepeare, though he speaks again and again of his deep wish to immortalise his friend, never names him?

2. The poem begins with the sustained simile comparing man's life to the sea breaking on the shingled shore, but the imagery in each quatrain is distinct and different. Trace this difference. Does Shakespeare succeed in making man's life seem more unattractive as you read through the three quatrains? Which descriptions of Time do you find most effective? Why?

3. Without the couplet this poem would end on a resigned and pessimistic note. How does Shakespeare counteract that pessimism in his concluding couplet?

4. Though intensely private, Sonnet 60 is also a general and universal utterance until the more personal references, 'my verse' and 'thy worth', in lines 13 and 14. How would you describe Shakespeare's mood here?

5. William Hazlitt (1778 – 1830) said that 'If Shakespeare had written nothing but his sonnets . . . he would . . . have been assigned to the class of cold, artificial writers, who had no genuine sense of nature or passion.' Do you find this sonnet heartless and contrived?

Critical Commentary

In this sonnet the poet is intensely aware of impermanence; example after example is listed, but the poem ends with an contrasting example of permanence and immortality. The three quatrains offer image upon image of movement and change: the waves, our lives, everything that grows, come to an end.

In stanza one the waves are presented as an image of our own hastening lives; our lives involve never-ending effort, like the waves hastening towards the shore: 'In sequent toil all forwards do contend'. 'Toil' (work with effort) and 'contend' (meaning strive) convey an unattractive, laborious picture of life.

In stanza two the poet speaks of the newborn 'in the main of light': in other words the baby, at first, is in the great expanse or ocean of life, but with the passing of time the growing person's life is doomed. Time, once a generous giver, now confounds or destroys that which it gave. The image of the sea in the first quatrain is picked up again in the second: the individual in the ocean of light 'Crawls to maturity' and, when he achieves the crown of success, even then Time will work against him: 'Crooked eclipses 'gainst his glory fight'. Time, once a friend, has become the enemy. Man, should he achieve glory, is from the very moment of glory being destroyed.

Decay and death are mentioned more and more frequently in each quatrain. Words which suggest Time is the destroyer are 'fight' and 'confound' in the first two quatrains; in the third quatrain:

> Time doth transfix the flourish set on youth,
> And delves the parallels in beauty's brow,
> Feeds on the rarities of nature's truth,
> And nothing stands but for his scythe to mow

Time as destroyer is there in every line, each one containing an active verb of destruction: 'transfix' (meaning destroy); 'delves the parallels' (digs wrinkles); 'Feeds on' (is nourished by); 'mow' (cut down). These are specific examples of how Time destroys, and are therefore more powerful and effective than, say, the general statement of line 2.

Time becomes more and more threatening, so much so that the picture seems very grim and hopeless in the poet's resigned tone in line 12:

> And nothing stands but for his scythe to mow

The 'nothing' here is total, final, but the couplet introduces a note of hope. The 'And yet' with which the couplet begins is quietly confident. And, having accepted that 'nothing stands but for his scythe to mow, the words 'shall stand' express a confident contradiction. In future times the friend to whom the sonnet is addressed will be praised because the poem will outlive time. The final image in the poem - that of Time with a scythe in his cruel hand - allows harsh reality almost to dominate.

William Wordsworth

William Wordsworth (1770 – 1850)

William Wordsworth was born on 7 April 1770 in Cockermouth, Cumberland, a small town in the north west of England, in a region known as the Lake District. He had a happy, wild and free childhood and loved outdoor life. He loved fishing, skating, wandering. Wordsworth's childhood was happy, wild and free and in the following lines, quoted by every biographer, he paints a picture of his young self playing on the banks of the river Derwent which bordered their garden:

> I, a four year's child,
> A naked boy, among the silent pools
> Made one long bathing of a summer's day,
> Basked in the sun, or plunged into thy streams,
> Alternate, all a summer's day, or coursed
> Over the sandy fields, and dashed the flowers
> Of yellow grunsel; or, when the crag and hill,
> The woods, and distant Skiddaw's lofty height,
> Were bronzed with a deep radiance, stood alone
> A naked savage in the thunder-shower . . .

These lines are from *The Prelude* which Wordsworth completed in 1799, when he was twenty-nine. It was first published in 1805 but Wordsworth reworked and revised the poem until 1839 and the final version was published immediately after his death in 1850.

However, his mother died when he was eight and his father when Wordsworth was thirteen and he and his four siblings were cared for by relatives. At seventeen Wordsworth went to Cambridge University, where he spent more time socialising than studying, and was awarded a pass degree in 1791. He rejected a career in law and the church and told a friend 'I am doomed to be an idler throughout my whole life'. As a student he had travelled in continental Europe, sometimes walking twenty or thirty miles a day. The political situation in France interested him and he returned there after Cambridge. In Orleans he had a relationship with Annette Vallon and she gave birth to their child, Caroline, in 1792, after Wordsworth had left for England. Among his family and friends Wordsworth made no secret of his past and later, in 1802, married a childhood friend, Mary Hutchinson. Two months before he married, he returned to France where, at Calais, he met his daughter for the first time. His sonnet 'It is a beauteous evening, calm and free' remembers their meeting. Wordsworth lived most of his life in the Lake District where he was born and, though he lived until eighty, many think he had written his best poetry by the age of thirty-five. He visited continental Europe and in 1828 toured Ireland and visited many parts of the country, including Kenmare and Killarney. In 1846 Wordsworth was elected to the Royal Irish Academy. In later life he was conservative, a churchgoer, the opposite to what he had been as a young man. He died on 13 April 1850 and was buried in Grasmere churchyard, one of the most popular places of literary pilgrimage.

'She dwelt among the untrodden ways' (1799)
'It is a beauteous evening calm and free' (1802)
from *The Prelude* Book I – Skating (1799)

'She dwelt among the untrodden ways'

She dwelt among the untrodden ways
    Beside the springs of Dove,
A Maid whom there were none to praise
    And very few to love:

A violet by a mossy stone   5
    Half hidden from the eye!
— Fair as a star, when only one
    Is shining in the sky.

She lived unknown, and few could know
    When Lucy ceased to be;   10
But she is in her grave, and, oh,
    The difference to me!

Glossary

1 dwelt: lived
1 untrodden ways: paths and walkways that are seldom used
2 springs of Dove: small streams at Dove – which, as Margaret Drabble points out, is not a real place.
3 Maid: girl, young woman

This lyric poem was composed in 1799 and is one of the five 'Lucy Poems'

Questions

1. This short lyric tells of Lucy's life and death. Tell the story in your own words. How does it differ from Wordsworth's? How different would the poem be if stanza two were omitted?

2. How much do we learn about Lucy in this poem? What does Wordsworth choose to tell us about the girl? Comment on the images of the violet and star. What do such images suggest about Lucy?

3. How does Wordsworth feel about Lucy? How would you describe his mood? Which words are most effective in conveying Wordsworth's mood, do you think?

4. Wordsworth uses end-rhyme in this lyric poem (abab). Comment on its effect.

5. Does Lucy, as she is portrayed in the poem, strike you as a real person? An interesting person? Give reasons for your answer.

6. What part does time play in this poem? Is time viewed here in a similar or different way from other poems by Wordsworth on your course?

Critical Commentary

This poem tells, in twelve lines, of the life and death of Lucy. 'She lived off the beaten track; she was not well-known; and now that she is dead the poet misses her very much' is how a summary of the poem would read. But the poem contains so much more.

The poet tells us very little about her, it would seem. Margaret Drabble says that there is a sense of vagueness, that Wordsworth 'tells us nothing practical, nothing factual about her at all. Even the "springs of Dove" that she dwelled beside are not a real place, which is odd only when one remembers what a passion Wordsworth had for using real places and real place names, and for giving his stories a detailed physical setting'.

And yet we have a strong sense of Lucy from the images in stanza two. Imagery here is not decorative. Lucy is a violet and she is a star. These metaphors are developed and elaborated and link Lucy to both earth and sky. The violet, a small and beautiful flower, is hardly seen; it is hidden. The star is all the more bright and special because it is the only one that can be seen:

> A violet by a mossy stone
> > Half hidden from the eye!
> —Fair as a star, when only one
> > Is shining in the sky.

The violet is hardly noticed, the star stands out and both qualities are attributed to Lucy.

The poem presents no difficulty in terms of meaning but the poem's power and success can be found in the music it makes and the intense feelings that it expresses. The rhyme and rhythm are regular; the exclamation marks add intensity and the very simple vocabulary suits Lucy's life and nature.

The final two lines are particularly effective. Her death is somehow indicated in the use of the past tense in the opening line ('lived') but the punctuation and the predominantly monosyllabic words give the closing lines a depth of feeling:

> But she is in her grave, and, oh,
> > The difference to me!

The world does not know of Lucy's death but her death has made the world of difference to the speaker.

'It is a beauteous evening, calm and free'

It is a beauteous evening, calm and free,
The holy time is quiet as a Nun
Breathless with adoration; the broad sun
Is sinking down in its tranquillity;
The gentleness of heaven broods o'er the Sea: 5
Listen! the mighty Being is awake,
And doth with his eternal motion make
A sound like thunder—everlastingly.
Dear Child! dear Girl! that walkest with me here,
If thou appear untouched by solemn thought,   10
Thy nature is not therefore less divine:
Thou liest in Abraham's bosom all the year;
And worshipp'st at the Temple's inner shrine,
God being with thee when we know it not.

Glossary

1 free: open, unconfined
5 broods: meditates silently
9 Dear Child! dear Girl!: Wordsworth's nine-year-old daughter, Caroline
12 Abraham's bosom: the repose of the happy in death; in Luke xvi .22 there is a reference to the soul's final resting place in heaven – 'And it came to pass, that the beggar died, and was carried by the angels into Abraham's bosom'.
13 Temple's inner shrine: the Temple is a sacred enclosure, the inner shrine was only entered by the sacred priests

Wordsworth wrote this sonnet in Calais in August 1802 when he and his sister Dorothy went to France to see Annette Vallon, with whom he was involved years earlier, and their daughter Caroline. Dorothy, in her Journals gives this account: 'The weather was very hot. We walked by the sea-shore almost every evening with Annette and Caroline or Wm and I alone...we had delightful walks after the heat of the day was passed away—seeing far off in the west the Coast of England.... The Evening star and the glory of the sky. The Reflections in the water were more beautiful than the sky itself, purple waves brighter than precious stones for ever melting away upon the sands.'

Questions

1. What is usually associated with evening? What aspects of evening does Wordsworth focus on in this sonnet? Pick out the details which best create, in your opinion, that evening scene. Comment on the use of sight and sound in the poem. Comment on the word 'broods'.

2. Trace the religious and spiritual references through the poem. What do such references suggest?

3. How would you describe the rhythm of the first five lines? What change takes place with 'Listen!' in line six? What is Wordsworth's tone here? How would you describe the poet's mood?

4. How would you describe the poet's choice of words? Why do you think he uses words such as 'beauteous', 'doth', 'Thou liest'?

5. 'Tintern Abbey' ends with Wordsworth's address to his sister. This sonnet ends with Wordsworth addressing his daughter. How do the poems compare and contrast in terms of what Wordsworth says to both?

6. Is this a usual or an unusual father/daughter poem? Give reasons for your answer.

7. Why is nature so important to Wordsworth as revealed to us in this poem?

8. Which of the poem's two sections, the octet or the sestet, do you prefer? Give reasons for your answer.

9. How does the child's reaction to the 'beauteous evening' differ from Wordsworth's? How does the poet view the child's response?

Critical Commentary

This sonnet was written in France in August 1802, when Wordsworth was thirty-two, and it is addressed to his nine-year-old daughter Caroline. The first eight lines describe the beautiful evening sunset and evening atmosphere; the remaining six lines focus on the relationship between the child and nature.

In the opening lines, in every line, many of the words suggest a great stillness:

> It is a beauteous evening, **calm** and free,
> The holy time is **quiet** as a Nun
> **Breathless** with adoration; the broad sun
> Is **sinking down** in its **tranquillity**;
> The **gentleness** of heaven **broods** o'er the Sea:

The time is 'holy' and the image of the Nun and the reference to heaven contribute to this sense of spirituality that Wordsworth recognises in the setting sun. These opening lines move slowly; the rhythm in this long, flowing sentence creates a solemn mood. The open vowel sounds in words such as 'calm', 'holy', 'adoration', 'broad', 'down', 'broods' create a stately music. The end rhymes also contribute to the harmony created within these lines: free/ Nun/ sun/ tranquillity/ Sea.

With line six there is a different music. The one word Listen with exclamation mark announces a new tone. Here Wordsworth is asking his daughter to listen to the sound of silence, for in the silence can be heard the mighty Being:

> Listen! the mighty Being is awake,
> And doth with his eternal motion make
> A sound like thunder—everlastingly.

In these lines Wordsworth achieves a sound that increases gradually and builds towards a crescendo. The poet senses a presence in the evening atmosphere. That this mighty Being is seen as having 'eternal motion' would suggest that for Wordsworth this Being is God and God in nature. That the sound he hears is compared to thunder suggests God's power and might.

The closing six lines or sestet move from the vast panorama of the evening sky and sea to the figure of the small child beside him. He does not address his daughter by name (even though 'Dear Caroline' would scan perfectly well in place of 'Dear Child! dear Girl!') and by calling her child and girl he is, in effect, speaking to all children. His feelings for her are intense – 'Dear Child! dear Girl!' – and, though he recognises that she does not respond to nature in the way that he does, if she does not have solemn thoughts on this occasion, it does not mean that she is untouched by the divine. Wordsworth believes his daughter is very close to God:

> Thou liest in Abraham's bosom all the year

In the Bible, Abraham's bosom is associated with a final resting place in heaven and perhaps Wordsworth is suggesting that his daughter beside him and all children are always close to heaven. In his poem 'Intimations of Immortality' Wordsworth says that 'Our birth is but a sleep and a forgetting' and that when we are born 'we come/ From God, who is our home'.

His daughter's special qualities are also found in the line which tells of how she

> worshipp'st at the Temple's inner shrine

which is a sacred enclosure where only sacred priests worshipped. These Christian references are clearly important to Wordsworth in this poem, which is not only a celebration of nature and God's presence but a blessing on his daughter.

The poem's closing line sums up something central to Wordsworth's understanding. In the opening lines he recognised God's presence but God can also be present even without our knowing it when we are with nature.

The words 'beauteous' in line one, 'doth' in line seven, and 'Thy' and 'Thou liest' belong to an earlier vocabulary than Wordsworth's. It resembles the language of the Bible and lends the sonnet an added dignity and solemnity.

from *The Prelude* Book 1
Childhood and School-time (lines 425-463)

Skating

And in the frosty season, when the sun
Was set, and visible for many a mile
The cottage windows blazed through twilight gloom,
I heeded not their summons: happy time
It was indeed for all of us—for me   5
It was a time of rapture! Clear and loud
The village clock tolled six,—I wheeled about,
Proud and exulting like an untired horse
That cares not for his home. All shod with steel,
We hissed along the polished ice in games   10
Confederate, imitative of the chase
And woodland pleasures,—the resounding horn,
The pack loud chiming, and the hunted hare.
So through the darkness and the cold we flew,
And not a voice was idle; with the din   15
Smitten, the precipices rang aloud;
The leafless trees and every icy crag
Tinkled like iron; while far distant hills
Into the tumult sent an alien sound
Of melancholy not unnoticed, while the stars   20
Eastward were sparkling clear, and in the west
The orange sky of evening died away.
Not seldom from the uproar I retired
Into a silent bay, or sportively
Glanced sideway, leaving the tumultuous throng,   25
To cut across the reflex of a star
That fled, and, flying still before me, gleamed
Upon the glassy plain; and oftentimes,
When we had given our bodies to the wind,
And all the shadowy banks on either side   30
Came sweeping through the darkness, spinning still
The rapid line of motion, then at once
Have I, reclining back upon my heels,
Stopped short; yet still the solitary cliffs
Wheeled by me—even as if the earth had rolled   35
With visible motion her diurnal round!
Behind me did they stretch in solemn train,
Feebler and feebler, and I stood and watched
Till all was tranquil as a dreamless sleep.

191

Glossary

4 heeded not: ignored, paid no attention to
4 summons: call
7 wheeled: turned with a revolving motion
8 exulting: rejoicing
11 Confederate: bound together
15 din: loud noise
16 Smitten: struck
16 precipices: steep cliffs
19 tumult: noise, uproar
19 alien: different
23 Not seldom: Frequently
24 sportively: playfully
25 glanced: moved rapidly
25 tumultuous: noisy
26 reflex: reflection
36 diurnal: daily
37 train: succession

Questions

1. 'The most immediately impressive thing about this passage is of course its amazing vitality', says Margaret Drabble. 'It is full of noise and movement and colour'. Which words best capture the noise, the movement, the colour? How does Wordsworth create the sense of winter, boyish gusto and the excitement and the rhythms of ice-skating in this passage? Pick out the words, phrases, images which, in your opinion, best capture the sensation.

2. Wordsworth makes you see; he also makes you hear. Examine the various sounds within the poem and their effect. What do you understand by 'an alien sound of melancholy'?

3. In lines 8-9 the poet compares his boyhood self to an untired horse. Do you think it an effective simile? Why? Why not?

4. There is a mood of exhilaration in the opening lines. How would you describe the mood in line 23 onward?

5. 'We hissed along the polished ice in games', writes Wordsworth in line ten. Is this a 'We' or an 'I' poem? Is Wordsworth part of a group or does he see himself as one apart?

6. How would you describe the relationship between Wordsworth and nature in this poem? Can the same be said of the other poems by Wordsworth on your course?

Critical Commentary

This is a memorable moment from boyhood which the twenty-nine-year-old adult Wordsworth remembers and describes in an atmospheric and vivid way. The opening lines involve the senses. We imagine that we feel the cold, see the setting sun, see the warm glow of the cottage windows and feel their warmth:

> And in the frosty season, when the sun
> Was set, and visible for many a mile
> The cottage windows blazed through twilight gloom . . .

Here the outdoor life means excitement and freedom. Though it is getting dark, Wordsworth is not thinking of going indoors. Though the cottage windows call, Wordsworth tells us that

> I heeded not their summons

He expresses his own individual delight when he speaks of how happy all children are in such a season but he particularly enjoys it:

> happy time
> It was indeed for all of us—-for me
> It was a time for rapture!

yet, when he describes the skating, he uses 'we', which gives the experience a feeling of togetherness. The body in movement and the thrill of skating on the frozen lake are expertly captured. The rhythms, the verbs and the images all contribute to this overall effect. In the dictionary, 'kinaesthesia' is defined as 'a sense of movement and muscular effort' and these lines certainly have that kinetic quality. This rapturous time is signalled first by the sound of bells, then by the energetic 'wheeled', Proud', 'Exulting', the simile of the 'untired horse':

> Clear and loud
> The village clock tolled six,—I wheeled about,
> Proud and exulting like an untired horse
> That cares not for its home . . .

The age-old and ever-effective techniques of alliteration ['**sh**od with **s**teel'] and onomatopoeia ['hissed'] and the comparison of the group of vocal skaters to the hunt makes for a very alive and dramatic scene:

> All shod with steel
> We hissed along the polished ice in games
> Confederate

The strong feeling of togetherness is emphasised in Wordsworth's use of confederate [meaning grouped or leagued together] and, in Wordsworth's mind, the skaters become a loud pack of hounds chasing a hare to the sounds of the hunting, echoing horn:

> imitative of the chase
> And woodland pleasures,—the resounding horn,
> The pack loud chiming, and the hunted hare.

The poetry gathers greater momentum as the skating is being described. The sounds are crisp, metallic and echoing and, in the midst of this excitement and tumult, Wordsworth senses a different mood, 'an alien sound/ Of melancholy'. This is the sound of the 'far distant hills' which into the tumult sent this melancholic alien sound. Such an interaction between man and nature is frequently found in Wordsworth's poetry. The others, however, do not sense it, seem not to notice, and Wordsworth, having entered into the spirit of the fun and the exhilaration of skating, withdraws frequently ('not seldom') and becomes more reflective:

> while the stars
> Eastward were sparkling clear, and in the west
> The orange sky of evening died away.
> Not seldom from the uproar I retired
> Into a silent bay, or sportively
> Glanced sideway, leaving the tumultuous throng,
> To cut across the reflex of a star
> That fled, and, flying still before me, gleamed
> Upon the glassy plain

The sense of camaraderie, comradeship, is changing here. The 'I' voice, not the communal 'we', is beginning to be heard in these lines when Wordsworth mentions that 'I retired' and in the remaining lines of the extract there is a growing sense of the individual self who gives himself to the wind and the earth's motion and moves towards an extraordinary stillness and a tranquil state:

> and oftentimes,
> When we have given our bodies to the wind
> And all the shadowy banks on either side
> Came sweeping through the darkness, spinning still
> The rapid line of motion, then at once
> Have I, reclining back upon my heels,
> Stopped short; yet still the solitary cliffs
> Wheeled by me—even as if the earth had rolled
> With visible motion her diurnal round!

The lines have great force and energy ('sweeping', 'spinning', 'wheeled', 'rolled') and the speaker feels at one with the earth's diurnal round. Seamus Heaney comments that 'The exhilaration of the skating, the vitality of the verbs, "gleaming", "sweeping", "spinning", "wheeling", the narrative push, the *cheerfulness*, to use one of the poet's favourite positive words—all these things have their part to play in the overall effect of the writing'.

There is a heightened sense of excitement, but also of understanding, and the poem's closing lines achieve a calm communion between the observer and the observed, between Wordsworth and nature. He thinks of the 'solitary cliffs' and how

> Behind me did they stretch in solemn train,
> Feebler and feebler, and I stood and watched
> Till all was tranquil as a dreamless sleep.

The opening lines were not 'tranquil' and far from sleep but the poem has journeyed from energetic boyhood to the calm, quiet, mature understanding of the close.

Of the Skating episode from *The Prelude*, John F. Danby says: 'It is an experience of tumultuous excitement, and yet precisely controlled, verbally given. The foot goes into the hollow of 'shod', re-echoing against the feel of steel, and then the hiss and kiss and swish of the polished ice (with its cry of delight) in the games.... There is every kind of concerted noise and motion, all issuing into a final silence.'

PART III
THE UNSEEN
POEM

The Poem on the Page

Every poem, to begin with, is an unseen poem. In your Leaving Certificate you will be asked to answer two poetry questions on paper two: one on the prescribed poets, one on an unseen poem. When approaching the unseen poem it is useful to ask some very basic questions, such as

- Who is speaking in the poem?
- What is being said?
- What prompted the poet to write the poem?
- What struck you first about this particular poem?
- What do you think of the opening? The ending?
- Does the poet use repetition?

The following is an outline of a step by step approach to the unseen poem on the page.

The Shape of the Poem on the Page

This is often the very first thing you will notice about the text. Certain forms are recognised immediately, for example the fourteen-lined sonnet. The American poet John Hollander is very interested in shape. His poem 'Swan and Shadow' would lose its impact if it were printed as follows:

Dusk Above the water hang the loud flies Here O so gray then What A pale signal will appear When Soon before its shadow fades Where Here in this pool of opened eye In us No Upon us As at the very edges of where we take shape in the dark air this object bares its image awakening ripples of recognition that will brush darkness up into light even after this bird this hour both drift by atop the perfect sad instant now already passing out of sight toward yet untroubled reflection this image bears its object darkening into memorial shades Scattered bits of light No of water Or something across water Breaking up No Being regathered soon Yet by then a swan will have gone Yes out of mind into what vast pale hush of a place past sudden dark as if a swan sang

This is how it should be:

Swan and Shadow

```
                      Dusk
                   Above  the
                water hang the
                      loud
                      flies
                      Here
                      O so
                      gray
                      then
                      What                 A pale signal will appear
                      When              Soon before its shadow fades
                      Where           Here in this pool of opened eye
                      In us      No Upon us As at the very edges
                   of where we take shape in the dark air
                      this object bares its image awakening
                      ripples of recognition that will
                         brush darkness up into light
    even after this bird this hour both drift by atop the perfect sad instant now
                      already passing out of sight
                      toward yet untroubled reflection
                      this image bears its object darkening
                      into memorial shades Scattered bits of
                      light       No of water Or something across
                      water         Breaking up No Being regathered
                      soon            Yet by then a swan will have
                      gone               Yes out of mind into what
                      vast
                      pale
                      hush
                      of a
                      place
                      past
                   sudden dark as
                      if a swan
                      sang
```

Shape here is so obviously of particular importance, but every poem has been shaped in a special way by means of line number, line length, rhyme and so on. Shakespeare wrote a 154 sonnet sequence; when Romeo and Juliet meet for the very first time in Shakespeare's play they speak a sonnet between them.

The Title

After the look of the poem on the page, this is the next thing that one notices. There is almost always a title. What does the choice of title tell us about the poem? When we get to know the poem better we can then think about how effective the title is.

Consider the following titles. What do they reveal, not reveal, suggest, imply, announce? Does the title win the reader's attention?

'The Dream of Wearing Shorts Forever' (Les Murray); 'Red Roses' (Anne Sexton); 'Red Sauce, Whiskey and Snow' (August Kleinzahler); 'Death of an Irishwoman' (Michael Hartnett); 'Hitcher' (Simon Armitage); 'Fifteen Million Plastic Bags' (Adrian Mitchell); 'For Heidi with Blue Hair' (Fleur Adcock); 'Wanting a Child' (Jorie Graham); 'SOMETHING FOR EVERYONE!!!' (Peter Reading); 'Phenomenal Woman' (Maya Angelou); 'The Hunchback in the Park' (Dylan Thomas); 'Going Home to Mayo, Winter, 1949' (Paul Durcan) ; 'To Autumn' (John Keats) ; 'This Moment' (Eavan Boland); 'Filling Station' (Elizabeth Bishop); [r-p-o-p-h-e-s-s-a-gr] (E E Cummings); 'The Forge' (Seamus Heaney); 'The Explosion' (Philip Larkin); 'From a Conversation During Divorce' (Carol Rumens); 'Wounds' (Michael Longley).

Language / Vocabulary

The language of poetry is the language of the age in which the poem is written. If someone today wrote a poem using "thee" and "thou" it would not convince; if someone today wrote exactly as Keats did that poem would be dismissed as inauthentic. The twentieth century poet writes in a language that is different from his or her predecessors. The poet today is less restricted in terms of subject matter. There is no word today, no emotion, no topic deemed unsuitable for poetry. Sylvia Plath said that she wanted to get the word 'toothbrush' into a poem, meaning that there was nothing too ordinary or mundane for the poet to write about.

Yet the magic of poetry is such that each of the poets in this collection, though they span four centuries and all write in the one language, has a distinctive, unique voice. Their very choice of words is part of this unique quality.

Ask yourself how you would describe a poet's vocabulary, his or her choice of words? This may be difficult to do at first. The task is easier if you look at opposites: Is the language unusual or ordinary? Formal or colloquial? Does the poet invent new words? and if so what does this tell us about the poet? Is the language concrete or abstract? Are the words drawn from Anglo-Saxon, Latin, Anglo-Irish? Are there words on the page drawn from the world of Greek Myth / Science / The Bible? Are there particular words that you would associate with particular poets? By asking such questions, you begin to develop an awareness of language and this will allow you to find a way to describe it.

The following illustrates some interesting differences between the language of prose and the language of poetry. The first is a newspaper article which, according to his biographer Lawrance Thompson, inspired Robert Frost's poem 'Out, Out –'. The second is the poem itself. A discussion of the similarities and differences between the two should sharpen an awareness of language.

from *The Littleton Courier*, 31 March 1901
Sad tragedy at Bethlehem
Raymond Fitzgerald, a Victim of fatal accident

Raymond Tracy Fitzgerald, one of the twin sons of Michael G. and Margaret Fitzgerald of Bethlehem, died at his home Thursday afternoon, March 24, as a result of an accident by which one of his hands was badly hurt in a sawing machine. The young man was assisting in sawing up some wood in his own dooryard with a sawing machine and accidently hit the loose pulley, causing the saw to descend upon his hand, cutting and lacerating it badly. Raymond was taken into the house and a physician was immediately summoned, but he died very suddenly from the effect of the shock, which produced heart failure . . . .

'Out, Out —'

The buzz saw snarled and rattled in the yard
And made dust and dropped stove-length sticks of wood,
Sweet-scented stuff when the breeze drew across it.
And from there those that lifted eyes could count
Five mountain ranges one behind the other
Under the sunset far into Vermont.
And the saw snarled and rattled, snarled and rattled,
As it ran light, or had to bear a load.
And nothing happened: day was all but done.
Call it a day, I wish they might have said
To please the boy by giving him the half hour
That a boy counts so much when saved from work.
His sister stood beside them in her apron
To tell them 'Supper'. At the word, the saw,
As if to prove saws knew what supper meant,
Leaped out at the boy's hand, or seemed to leap —
He must have given the hand. However it was,
Neither refused the meeting. But the hand!
The boy's first outcry was a rueful laugh,
As he swung toward them holding up the hand
Half in appeal, bit half as if to keep
The life from spilling. Then the boy saw all —
Since he was old enough to know, big boy
Doing a man's work, though a child at heart —
He saw all spoiled. 'Don't let him cut my hand off —

The doctor, when he comes. Don't let him, sister!'
So. But the hand was gone already.
The doctor put him in the dark of ether.
He lay and puffed his lips out with his breath.
And then—the watcher at his pulse took fright.
No one believed. They listened at his heart.
Little — less— nothing! — and that ended it.
No more to build on there. And they, since they
Were not the one dead, turned to their affairs.

Punctuation

All poets are wordsmiths and punctuation is an aspect essential to poetry. Sometimes its absence is deliberate, as in the poems by Emily Dickinson. The frequent use of the full-stop will naturally slow down a line. The full-stop, the comma, the colon, the exclamation mark, the question mark, the dash, the bracket, dots and the use of italics are just some aspects of punctuation, and all are important aspects of a writer's style. Why does one of the poems by Emily Dickinson on your course end with a full-stop, the other with a dash?

Rhyme

Rhyme, for centuries, has been one of the most distinguishing characteristics of poetry, though a poetry without a regular rhyming scheme is not necessarily a poetry without music. Blank verse, which is unrhymed iambic pentameter, for example, achieves rhythm and cadence without end rhyme. Internal rhyme and cross rhyme are also important features in poetry. The run-on line is deceptive in that often a very rigorous and regular rhyming scheme is not apparent.

Rhythm

Rhythm is movement. We are all familiar with rhythm. The individual day, the seasons of the year, the sound of the sea all have their own rhythm or movement. The poet Paula Meehan believes that our sense of rhythm dates from the time spent in our mother's womb – the regular heartbeat of the mother and our own heartbeat give us an inbuilt rhythmic pattern.

Cadence

Of the three concepts rhyme, rhythm and cadence, cadence is the most difficult to define, yet it is easily recognised. A dictionary definition speaks of the rise and fall of words. If you consider the following short extracts you can hear this rising, falling sound, and it is a very effective means of capturing a mood:

It was evening all afternoon.
It was snowing
And it was going to snow.
(from 'Thirteen Ways of Looking at a Blackbird' by Wallace
Stevens)

Only the groom, and the groom's boy,
With bridles in the evening come.

(from 'At Grass' by Philip Larkin)

The cadence here creates a mood: in the first, a melancholy one; in
the second, a peaceful, tranquil one. The sounds of the words, the
arrangement of the words in the line and the use of repetition, for
example, create these cadences.

Line Break and Line Length

These are other important aspects of the total impact of the poem. [It
would be a worthwhile and interesting exercise to think about line break
in a poem you are not already familiar with. Here are three poems, two
by William Carlos Williams and one by Eavan Boland. How do you think
they ought to be arranged on the page?

the red wheelbarrow
so much depends upon a red wheelbarrow glazed with rain
water beside the white chickens

to a poor old woman
munching a plum on the street a paper bag of them in her hand
they taste good to her they taste good to her they taste good
to her you can see it by the way she gives herself to the one
half sucked out in her hand comforted a solace of ripe plums
seeming to fill the air they taste good to her

[Compare and contrast your versions with the poems printed in Appendix
II, page 221.]

Imagery

If you say the words traffic-jam, strobe lighting, town, river, hillside,
elephant, images form one after the other in your mind, all in a matter
of seconds. Many of the words in the English language conjure up an
image on their own. Every noun does, for example. However there is
a difference between the image prompted by the word 'tiger' and the
phrases 'roaring like a tiger' or 'he's a tiger'. Here tiger becomes simile
and metaphor. Symbol is another familiar and powerful technique, and
symbol occurs when something in the poem such as a tiger in a cage is
both actual and means something beyond itself. For example, a caged
animal is just that, but it can also stand for the death of freedom.

The Voice

TONE: What is being said and how it is being said are very important. Think for a moment of the sentence: 'Please leave the room'. Tone or the attitude of the speaker can make a huge difference here. First try saying that sentence four different ways simply by emphasising a different word each time. Then, if you introduce a note of anger or exhaustion or apathy or urgency into your voice, the sentence takes on a different meaning. In poetry tone is the attitude the poet / speaker has towards his / her listener / reader. Tone can be formal or casual/off-hand, serious or tongue-in-cheek, superior or prayer-like, profound or simple and so on.

MOOD: A tone can create a mood or atmosphere. Mood is the feeling contained within the work and the feeling communicated to the reader. In Eavan Boland's poem 'This Moment' the mood is one of expectation and mystery.

ALLUSION: This is when one writer refers to another writer's work, either directly or indirectly, and when an allusion is used it can enhance or enlarge a topic or it can serve as an effective contrast.

ONOMATOPOEIA: Listen out for the sounds. Read the poem aloud and the onomatopoeic words will clearly reveal themselves.

The Unseen Poem –
A Response

A Blessing

Just off the highway to Rochester, Minnesota,
Twilight bounds softly forth on the grass.
And the eyes of those two Indian ponies
Darken with kindness.
They have come gladly out of the willows   5
To welcome my friend and me.
We step over the barbed wire into the pasture
Where they have been grazing all day, alone.
They ripple tensely, they can hardly contain their happiness
That we have come.   10
They bow shyly as wet swans. They love each other.
There is no loneliness like theirs.
At home once more,
They begin munching the young tufts of spring in the darkness.
I would like to hold the slenderer one in my arms,   15
For she has walked over to me
And nuzzled my left hand.
She is black and white,
Her mane falls wild on her forehead,
And the light breeze moves me to caress her long ear   20
That is delicate as the skin over a girl's wrist.
Suddenly I realise
That if I stepped out of my body I would break
Into blossom.

James Wright (1927 – 1980)

As we ask ourselves, What have we here? It is important that we re-read the poem a few times. A poem usually consists of sentences or sections and, having read the poem through several times, it may be useful to approach the poem a sentence or a line or two at a time.

Here, he shape of the poem seems to be irregular. There is no obvious rhyming scheme. The poem contains twelve sentences, some long and flowing, others equally effective because they are short. The lines are of uneven length and the final line is the shortest.

Wright calls his poem 'A Blessing' not 'The Blessing' which would imply something more specific. If the moment that he writes about is 'a' blessing, it means that there are other such moments also. The blessing experienced in this particular moment, however, is the particular focus of this poem. A blessing has religious and holy connotations and it is a holy and special moment for the poet, though the setting is not a place associated with a conventional religious experience.

The poem begins in a matter-of-fact way: 'Just off the highway . . ' and the American city and State are named. A 'highway' suggests reinforced concrete, the man-made, busyness, speed, but the second line is soft and natural and beautiful, capturing, as it does, a world 'Just off the highway'. It is twilight, a time of fading light and shadows; the quaint, old-fashioned phrase 'softly forth' contains gentle sounds and the grass contrasts with the highway itself.

The use of the word 'And' at the beginning of line three, which is also the beginning of a new sentence, leads us further into the poem. The first thing that Wright tells us about the ponies is that their eyes 'darken with kindness' and that they are Indian ponies. Their mystery and their nature are conveyed in the words 'darken' and 'kindness'; that they are Indian may be significant. Modern America as symbolised by the highway is very different from the Native American / Indian tradition.

'Gladly' and 'welcome' suggest how Wright feels as both he and his friend are approached by the ponies.

The human and the animal world meet when 'We step over the barbed wire'. Wright speaks of the ponies being alone. Their happiness is vividly conveyed in a phrase: 'They ripple tensely'.

There is no sound mentioned. The image Wright uses – 'They bow shyly as wet swans' – is elegant and graceful and beautiful. The three short sentences in line 11–12, each following the other, are effective. They are both the poet's accurate observation and his conclusions:

> They bow shyly as wet swans. They love each other.
> There is no loneliness like theirs.

The loneliness which the poet speakes of here is a different kind of loneliness, a loneliness that does not frighten or destroy.

The moment passes and the ponies are 'At home once more', happy to be visited and happy to feel at ease 'munching the young tufts of spring in the darkness', a phrase which contains sensuous, evocative details.

The final part of the poem, the last three sentences, focuses on the speaker. 'I', absent from the poem so far, is now used four times. 'I would like to hold the slenderer one in my arms' is Wright's response when his left hand is nuzzled ['ripple';'munching';'nuzzle' add to the sensuousness of the experience]. It is clearly a very personal and beautiful moment that the poet is recording. He moves from the very emotional/subjective response to objective description in the lines:

> She is black and white,
> Her mane falls wild on her forehead

and returns again to the intense emotion of 'the light breeze moves me to caress her long ear'. The image of the 'skin over a girl's wrist' is echoing the earlier image of the swans. Both are graceful and slender and delicate. Then the moment of insight comes and it comes 'suddenly':

> Suddenly I realise
> That if I stepped out of my body I would break
> Into blossom.

The final image is inspired by the natural world and, just as a blossom unfolds naturally and beautifully, Wright, in choosing this image, is giving us a very vivid description of a complex, metaphysical/spiritual moment. It is a poem of longing and here the word 'break', so often associated with destruction, is used with opposite effect. The word 'break' is also placed appropriately at the line break.

•

The above is but a beginning but gradually, with each re-reading, you can enter more fully into the poem. If, for example, you focus on the mood of the poem would one word sum up the mood or does the mood change and how would you describe that changing mood? What is the dominant mood of this poem?

Are the verbs or adjectives or sound of particular importance? What if the images were removed? What would the poem lose?

Your own response to a poem on the page should focus on THEME and TECHNIQUE. Hundreds of poems may share a similar theme but every true poet has his or her own individual way of viewing and expressing an idea, his or her own individual way of mastering technique.

A selection of poems suited to the Unseen Poetry question at Ordinary Level

Advice to My Son

The trick is, to live your days,
as if each one may be your last
(for they go fast, and young men lose their lives
in strange and unimaginable ways)
but at the same time, plan long range   5
(for they go slow: if you survive
the sheltered windshield and the bursting shell
you will arrive
at our approximation here below
of heaven or hell).   10
To be specific, between the peony and the rose
plant squash and spinach, turnips and tomatoes;
beauty is nectar
and nectar, in a desert, saves —
but the stomach craves stronger sustenance   15
than the honied vine.
Therefore, marry a pretty girl
after seeing her mother;
show your soul to one man,
work with another,   20
and always serve bread with your wine.
But son,
always serve wine.

Peter Meinke

Read this poem slowly a number of times. Try to think about the pictures
it makes and the feelings those pictures give you. Don't be worried if you
cannot catch the full meaning of the poem; just talk about the parts that
have most meaning for you.

Questions

1. In lines 1-10 what line(s) give you the most powerful picture? Outline the picture and the feelings and ideas it brings. Is there any other place in the poem where those same feelings can be found? Write about those lines.

2. In your view does this poem give a sad view of life or a happy view of life or a mixture of the two? Explain your answer by selecting some lines to illustrate your viewpoint.

3. How would you describe the way the poem uses words? Choose from the following the phrases that describe the poem best for you:

  (a) like a friendly chat
  (b) like a sermon
  (c) like a serious message
  (d) like a song
  (e) like a set of friendly instructions

Choose some words and phrases from the poem to support your opinion.

4. Some phrases from the poem are like 'wise sayings' or 'proverbs'. e.g. 'plan long range', 'beauty is nectar'. Pick out some other phrases like this and write about what they bring to the poem.

July Day Spectacular

I sit in the third row of
gray rocks upholstered
with lichen. Light pours
from the flies of heaven
on a thirty mile stage-set;   5
and there, by the footlights
of breaking water,
oystercatchers,
going through their old routines,
put on their black-and-white minstrel show   10
watched by a bandmaster pigeon
with built in epaulettes.

Norman MacCaig

Questions

1. Read this poem a number of times and then decide how the poet feels about what he sees.

2. Choose some of the following words which you think would be appropriate to describe the scene in the poem as the poet presents it: lively, serious, dull, monotonous, entertaining, light-hearted. Could you suggest another word to describe the poet's viewpoint?

3. The poet is describing a seaside scene. To what does he compare it and what is the impact of the comparison?

4. Pick out some words in the poem which you found interesting and / or surprising and talk about them.

Eily Kilbride

On the north side of Cork city
Where I sported and played
On the banks of my own lovely Lee
Having seen the goat break loose in Grand Parade

I met a child, Eily Kilbride   5
Who'd never heard of marmalade,
Whose experience of breakfast
Was coldly limited,

Whose entire school day
Was a bag of crisps,   10
Whose parents had no work to do,

Who went, once, into the countryside,
Saw a horse with a feeding bag over its head
And thought it was sniffing glue.

Brendan Kennelly

Questions

1. In your view, why did the poet write this poem?

2. How does the poet feel about Eily? Choose at least two from the
following list of descriptive words which you think describe the way he is
feeling: sad, angry, gentle, happy, shocked, uncaring, frustrated. Explain
your choices.

3. The first verse includes a line from a popular and well-known song
about Cork, 'On the Banks of My Own Lovely Lee'. Why do you think that
line is included here?

4. What part of Eily's experience would you see as the most upsetting?
Explain your choice by describing the kind of picture it gives you and
the feelings related to it.

Did Anything Happen at the Field Today, Dear?

The photograph shows
the frozen horror at that moment in time
the airship
booming into flame
the people   5
tiny
running to and fro arms
raised in fright
and looking closer we can see
one person   10
unconcerned
walking from the field
not having noticed the panic
behind him
striding   15
hands in his pockets
head bowed
in thought
he walks away
admiring the splendid polish   20
of his boots

Richard Hill

Questions

Read this poem a number of times and, when you feel you have some
sense of it, attempt the following questions.

1. There are two different viewpoints on a certain moment given in this
poem, i.e. what the 'people' saw and what the 'person' saw. Describe
what each of these saw, according to the poem. What feelings and ideas
do these two pictures give?

2. Who do you think is talking to whom in the title of the poem? Explain
how the title hints at what the poem is about.

3. Select from the poem four phrases which, for you, carry the main
impact of the poem. Explain your choice.

4. From the list below choose the phrase which is very close to or very
different from your own reading of the text and explain your choice:
> (a) The two different viewpoints make the airship disaster seem
>   more sad and tragic.
> (b) The presence of two viewpoints means that the reader's
>   attention is drawn away from the airship disaster.
> (c) The poem makes people seem insignificant and unimportant.

Pot Roast

I gaze upon the roast,
that is sliced and laid out
on my plate
and over it
I spoon the juices   5
of carrot and onion.
And for once I do not regret
the passage of time.

I sit by a window
that looks   10
on the soot-stained brick of buildings
and do not care that I see
no living thing – not a bird,
not a branch in bloom,
not a soul moving   15
in the rooms
behind the dark panes.
These days when there is little
to love or to praise
one could do worse   20
than yield
to the power of food.
So I bend
to inhale
the steam that rises   25
from my plate, and I think
of the first time
I tasted a roast
like this
It was years ago   30
in Seabright.
Nova Scotia:
my mother leaned
over my dish and filled it
and when I finished   35
filled it again.
I remember the gravy,
its odour of garlic and celery,
and sopping it up
with pieces of bread.   40
And now
I taste it again.
The meat of memory
The meat of no change.
I raise my fork in praise,   45
And I eat.

Mark Strand

This is a poem which uses food and the memory of food in an interesting way. While sitting at a meal a person starts remembering other meals. Read the poem a few times and jot down whatever it suggests to you. Then respond to the following questions and proposals.

Questions

1. 'There are feelings of warmth and love here but also feelings of coldness and death.' What do you think? In your view which, finally, is the dominant feeling in the poem?

2. Since this poem describes eating, there should be sensuous words present in it. Select some words which created for you a sense of rich tastes, textures and scents.

3. At the end the poet raises his 'fork in praise'. Why does he do this? Is he praising food, meat, his mother, himself or what?

4. 'Poems can add rich meanings to the ordinary events of life?' Is this true of this poem?

Running on Empty

As a teenager I would drive Father's
Chevrolet cross-country, given me

reluctantly: 'Always keep the tank
half full, boy, half full, ya hear?'

The fuel gauge dipping, dipping   5
towards Empty, hitting Empty, then

— thrilling! — 'way below Empty,
myself driving cross-country

mile after mile, faster and faster,
all night long, this crazy kid driving   10

the earth's rolling surface,
against all laws, defying chemistry,

rules, and time, riding on nothing
but fumes, pushing luck harder

than anyone pushed before, the wind   15
screaming past like the Furies . . .

I stranded myself only once, a white
night with no gas station open, ninety miles

from nowhere. Panicked for a while
at standstill, myself stalled.   20

At dawn the car and I both refilled. But,
Father, I am running on empty still.

Robert Phillips

This poem apparently tells about an incident from the poet's teenage
years. Read it a few times to get a clear picture of what actually
happened. Having read it, note down any words that interest/surprise
you or any ideas, images and feelings it raised and then respond to the
following proposals and questions.

Questions

1. 'The poem is full of a sense of movement and risk.' Where in the poem can you find these feelings/ How is the language used to give that sense of movement?

2. Why did the poet take such pleasure in 'running on empty'? Choose some words and phrases which suggest his reasons.

3. What feeling does the last line create? Choose from the following words which match the line's impact on you: sad, happy, defiant, hopeless, helpless, angry, arrogant, bitter.

The Jaguar

The apes yawn and adore their fleas in the sun.
The parrots shriek as if they were on fire, or strut
Like cheap tarts to attract the stroller with the nut.
Fatigued with indolence, tiger and lion

Lie still as the sun. The boa-constrictor's coil   5
Is a fossil. Cage after cage seems empty, or
Stinks of sleepers from the breathing straw.
It might be painted on a nursery wall.

But who runs like the rest past these arrives
At a cage where the crowd stands, stares, mesmerized,   10
As a child at a dream, at a jaguar hurrying enraged
Through prison darkness after the drills of his eyes

On a short fierce fuse. Not in boredom—
The eye satisfied to be blind in fire,
By the bang of blood in the brain deaf the ear—   15
He spins from the bars, but there's no cage to him

More than to the visionary his cell:
His stride is wilderness of freedom:
The world rolls under the long thrust of his heel.
Over the cage floor the horizons come.   20

Ted Hughes

Questions

1. What is the atmosphere in the zoo in the first two stanzas of this poem? Which words best capture that atmosphere?

2. Why is the Jaguar singled out for special mention by the poet?

3. Which words in the poem create pictures of the jaguar in your head? Does Ted Hughes convince you that the Jaguar is special?

4. Comment on the final line of the poem.

Over and Over

Over and over they suffer, the gentle creatures,
The frightened deer, the mice in the corn to be gathered,
Over and over we cry, alone or together.
And we weep for a lot we scarcely understand,
Wondering why we are here and what we mean   5
And why there are huge stars and volcanic eruptions,
Earthquakes, desperate disasters of many kinds.
What is the answer? Is there

One? There are many. Most of us forget
The times when the going sun was a blaze of gold   10
And the blue hung behind it and we were the whole of awe,
We forget the moments of love and cast out time
And the children who come to us trusting the answers we give
To their difficult and important questions. And there

Are shooting stars and rainbows and broad blue seas.   15
Surely when we gather the good about us
The dark is cancelled out. Mysteries must
Be our way of life. Without them we might
Stop trying to learn and hoping to succeed
In the work we half-choose and giving the love we need.   20

Elizabeth Jennings

Questions

1. In your view what kind of a person wrote this poem? Give reasons for
your answer.

2. 'Mysteries must/ Be our way of life.' From this poem do you think that
Elizabeth Jennings believes in life's mysteries? Why?

3. Why do you think Elizabeth Jennings called her poem 'Over and Over'?

4. Do you think this a happy or a gloomy poem? Or is it a mixture of
both. Refer to the poem in your answer.

PART IV
APPENDICES
GLOSSARY
ACKNOWLEDGEMENTS

Appendix I

Responding to a poem

Some Questions to Ask:

- Who is speaking? (the poet?/ a persona?/ an inanimate object?/ an animal?)
- What is being said?
- What occasion prompted the poem/ why was it written?
- How does the poem begin?
- How does it end? (Write down the opening and closing lines and comment on the style)
- Which line/ section captures the gist of the poem?
- Which image is the most effective/ striking/ memorable?
- What struck you first about a particular poem?
- What struck you while re-reading the poem?
- Comment on the shape of the poem.
- Are the lines regular in length?
- Comment on the stanza divisions.
- Does the poem belong to a particular genre? – sonnet/sestina/ballad/lyric/epic/ode....?
- Comment on the punctuation in the poem. What would the page look like if only the punctuation remained? (e.g. poet's use of question marks, dashes, commas, and where these occur in the line)
- Ask if the poet uses (i) alliteration (ii) assonance (iii) onomatopoeia (iv) end-rhyme (v) internal rhyme (vi) metaphor (vii) simile (viii) repetition (ix) rhyme scheme (x) run-on lines
- Comment on the title of the poem.
- If you were to paint this poem, what colours would you use?
- If this poem were a piece of music how would you describe it? Which musical instrument(s) would suit it best?
- Draw three pictures or images which you see with your mind's eye when reading or thinking about this poem.
- Say from which source the poet has drawn these images – from nature, art, mythology, science . . . .
- Which is the most important word/line in the poem? Justify your choice.

Appendix II

Two poems by William Carlos Williams

The Red Wheelbarrow

so much depends
upon

a red wheel
barrow

glazed with rain
water

beside the white
chickens

To A Poor Old Woman

munching a plum on
the street a paper bag
of them in her hand

They taste good to her
They taste good
to her. They taste
good to her

You can see it by
the way she gives herself
to the one half
sucked out in her hand

Comforted
a solace of ripe plums
seeming to fill the air

Glossary of Literary Terms

ALLITERATION: when two or more words in close connection begin with the same letter or sound and affect the ear with an echoing sound. Examples include the childhood doggerel, 'Betty bought a bit of butter but the butter Betty bought was bitter'. Dickinson uses alliteration as in 'Berries of the Bahamas – have I – / But this little Blaze . . .'; or Larkin in 'The Whitsun Weddings' - 'A slow and stopping curve southwards we kept'; or Seamus Heaney's 'to the tick of two clocks'.

ALLUSION: this is when a writer deliberately introduces into his/her own work recognisable elements from another source. This may be a reference to a well-known character, event, or place or to another work of art. For example, in her poem 'Love', Eavan Boland never names Virgil's Aeneas but the reader is expected to identify 'the hero . . . on his way to hell' as an allusion to Book VI of *The Aeneid.*

AMBIGUITY: when language is open to one or more interpretations based on the context in which it occurs. Ambiguity can be intentional or unintentional. An example would be the opening line of Keats's 'Ode on a Grecian Urn': 'Thou still unravished bride of quietness' – where the word 'still' can mean 'without movement, silent' or 'as before, up to the present time'

ANAGRAM: this is when a rearrangement of the letters in one word or phrase results in a new word or phrase, as in 'listen' into 'silent', 'now' into 'won'.

ARCHAISM: in Greek the word means 'old-fashioned', and an archaism is when a writer or speaker deliberately uses a word or phrase no longer in current use, for example, 'oft', 'morn', 'thy'. Keats's use of 'faery' in 'Ode to a Nightingale' is an example.

ASSONANCE: In Latin 'assonare' is 'to answer with the same sound'. Assonance is when vowel sounds are repeated in a sequence of words close to each other. For example, in W. B. Yeats: 'I hear lake water lapping with low sounds by the shore'.

BALLAD: a simple and memorable song that tells a story in oral form through narrative and dialogue. It is one of the oldest forms of literature and was originally passed on orally among illiterate people. Ballads often tell of love, courage, the supernatural. Ballads usually are written in four-line stanzas with an abcb rhyme, and often have a refrain. The first and third lines are usually four stress iambic tetrameter, the second and fourth lines are in three stress iambic trimeter. For example:

> There lived a wife at Usher's Well
>
> And a wealthy wife was she
>
> She had three stout and stalwart sons,
>
> An sent them o'er the sea.

Other examples of ballad include Keats's 'La Belle Dame sans Merci' and the anonymous 'Frankie and Johnny'.

BLANK VERSE: this is unrhymed iambic pentameter and is often used in long poems and dramatic verse. One of the earliest examples of blank verse in English is to be found in Henry Howard Surrey's translation of Virgil's *Aeneid*, which was published in 1540. Shakespeare, Milton, Wordsworth, Robert Frost all wrote in blank verse.

CADENCE: the word 'cadence' means 'the fall of the voice' and refers to the last syllables in a pattern of words. Cadence is difficult to define, and yet it is easily identified or, more accurately, easily heard. When Philip Larkin writes at the end of 'At Grass'

> With bridles in the evening come

we know that the sounds have been arranged in a particularly effective way on the page. For example, he puts the verb at the end which is not usual in English (it is a Latin form), but the effect is musical and beautiful and very different from 'Come with bridles in the evening', which says exactly the same thing. Cadence is found especially in Biblical poetry, free verse, prose poetry. Ezra Pound in *Make It New* (1934) urged poets to 'compose in the sequence of the musical phrase, not in sequence of a metronome'.

CAESURA: a caesura is a pause which usually occurs in the middle of a line and is caused by rhyme, punctuation or syntax. For example Boland uses the caesura for effect in the closing lines of 'The Pomegranate':

> The legend will be hers as well as mine.
> She will enter it. As I have.
> She will wake up. She will hold
> the papery flushed skin in her hand.
> And to her lips. I will say nothing.

CARICATURE: from an Italian word meaning 'to exaggerate'. When a character's personality or physical feature is portrayed in a distorted manner the result is a caricature. The cartoonist's work is almost always a caricature.

CLICHÉ: a phrase which has through overuse become familiar and jaded. The word cliché originally referred to a plate used in printing which produced numerous identical copies. Clichés were once original and interesting uses of language but now, though it is difficult to do so, they are best avoided. Examples include 'a clear blue sky', 'go haywire', 'hard as a rock', 'stand up and be counted', 'tough as nails'.

CLIMAX: Climax comes from a Greek word meaning ladder and a climactic moment is one when there is intensity. In a Shakespearean play, for example, there is often a climax in Acts III and V, when the audience's interest is at its height. In Shelley's sonnet 'Ozymandias' the lines 'My name is Ozymandias, King of Kings,/ Look on my Works, ye Mighty, and despair!' form a climax.

CLOSURE: The way a poem, novel, play, etc. ends and how the author achieves the sense of an ending. For example, Shakespeare in his sonnets uses a rhyming couplet; Philip Larking in 'The Explosion' places a single line between eight three line stanzas.

COMPARATIVE LITERATURE: the study of the relationships and similarities between different literatures by writers from different nations or peoples – e.g. you can read *Great Expectations* by Charles Dickens and *Cat's Eye* by Margaret Atwood and examine and analyse both as 'coming of age' novels or Bildungsroman (an upbringing or education novel) – one about a boy in the nineteenth-century in England, the other about a girl growing up in Canada in the twentieth. Ian Reed states that 'Unless we compare things, we cannot see things either wholly or fully'; and Michael Lapidge says: 'The comparative approach is instinctive to human intelligence. From our very infancy we learn by comparing like with like, and by distinguishing the like from the nearly like, and the other.'

COUPLET: two lines of rhymed or unrhymed verse which follow the same metre. Eavan Boland's 'The War Horse' is written in couplets. The heroic couplet is made up of iambic pentameter lines which rhyme in pairs.

CRITICISM: the evaluation, interpretation and discussion of a work

CROSS RHYME: (or interlaced rhyme) this occurs when a word at the end of a line rhymes with a word in the middle of a following line.

ELEGY: Elegy comes from the Greek word meaning lament. The elegy is usually a long, formal poem which mourns the dead. Gray's 'Elegy in a Country Churchyard' is one of the more famous. Also, Whitman's elegy for Abraham Lincoln, 'When Lilacs Last in the Dooryard Bloom'd' and W. H. Auden's 'In Memory of W.B. Yeats'.

END RHYME: this is when the words at the end of lines rhyme

ENJAMBMENT: also known as the run-on line, enjambment occurs when a line ending is not end stopped but flows into the following line. For example these lines from Michael Longley's 'The Greengrocer':

> He ran a good shop, and he died
> Serving even the death-dealers
> Who found him busy as usual
> Behind the counter, organised
> With holly wreaths for Christmas,
> Fir trees on the pavement outside.

EPIGRAM: a short witty well-made poem. Coleridge defined the epigram as follows and the definition is itself an epigram.

> 'What is an epigram? A dwarfish whole
> Its body brevity, and wit its soul'

Another example would be the epigram called 'Coward' by A. R. Ammons: 'Bravery runs in my family.'

EPIPHANY: A moment of illumination, beauty, insight. For example, the closing lines of Elizabeth Bishop's 'The Fish' or the final stanza of Seamus Heaney's 'Sunlight'.

EYE RHYME: (also known as sight-rhyme) eye-rhyme occurs when two words or the final parts of the words are spelled alike, but have different pronunciations as in 'tough/bough', 'blood/mood'.

FOOT: a metrical unit of measurement in verse and the line can be divided into different numbers of feet as follows:

one-foot line	:	monometer
two-foot line	:	dimeter
three-foot line	:	trimeter
four-foot line	:	tetrameter
five-foot line	:	pentameter
six-foot line	:	hexameter
seven-foot line	:	heptameter
eight-foot line	:	octameter

Once a line is divided into feet, each foot can then be identified as containing a distinctive metrical pattern. For example, if a foot contain one weak and one strong stress (U –) that foot is an iamb or an iambic foot. If there are five iambic feet in a line it is known as an iambic pentameter. The following are the most common forms of metrical foot – the stress pattern is given and an example:

iamb (iambic)	:	U – (hello)
rochee (trochaic)	:	– U (only; Wallace; Stevens)
anapest (anapestic)	:	U U – (understand)
dactyl (dactylic)	:	– U U (suddenly; Emily; Dickinson)
spondee (spondaic)	:	– – (deep peace)

FREE VERSE: on the page free verse is unrhymed, often follows an irregular line length and line pattern and is unmetered. Free verse depends on rhythm, repetition or unusual typographical and grammatical devices for effect.

FULL RHYME: (also known as perfect rhyme or true rhyme) when the sound or sounds in one word are perfectly matched by the sounds in another. For example soon and moon, thing/spring, mad/bad, head/said, people/steeple, curious/furious, combination/domination.

HALF RHYME: (also called slant-rhyme, near-rhyme, off-rhyme, half-rhyme, partial rhyme, imperfect rhyme) half-rhyme occurs when two words have certain sound similarities, but do not have perfect rhymes. Half-rhymes often depend on the same last consonant in two words such as 'blood' and 'good' or 'poem' and 'rum'. Emily Dickinson, Hopkins, Yeats, Dylan Thomas, Elizabeth Bishop and many other poets use half-rhyme.

HYPERBOLE: in Greek the word 'hyperbole' means 'an overshooting, an excess' and hyperbole is the deliberate use of exaggeration or overstatement for dramatic or comic effect. For example in 'The Daffodils' Wordsworth is using hyperbole in 'Ten thousand saw I at a glance'. The opposite of hyperbole is litotes.

IAMB: the iamb is a metrical foot made up of one unaccented syllable followed by an accented one (⌣ –). The word 'today' or 'forget' or 'hello' are examples of the iamb.

IAMBIC PENTAMETER: the word pentameter is Greek for five measures and is used to describe a line of verse containing five metrical feet. The iambic pentameter is the most commonly used meter in the English language and there's a very simple reason for this: the length of an iambic pentameter line is the length of time most of us can hold our breath. Blank verse, which Shakespeare used in his plays, is unrhymed iambic pentameter. There is a old girls' skipping chant which goes 'I must, I must, I must, improve my bust' and it is a perfect example of iambic pentameter. So too is a sentence such as 'You make me sick, you make me really sick' or 'My birthday is the twenty-sixth of May'. The iambic pentameter could be represented as follows:

daDA daDA daDA daDA daDA or (⌣ – | ⌣ – | ⌣ – | ⌣ – | ⌣ –)

Obviously, when you read a line of iambic pentameter, you do not exaggerate the stress, just as we do not exaggerate the stress on a vowel sound in our everyday speech. In the poem, however, the underlying structured pattern creates a music and a flow that is heard in the ear. If you look at and read lines such as the following from Eavan Boland's 'The Pomegranate', you will see and hear them as iambic pentameters:

I climb the stairs and stand where I can see (line 26)

The rain is cold. The road is flint-coloured (line 43)

Not every line in a poem which is written in iambic pentameter will follow the iambic pentameter pattern. If that were the case, the sequence of stresses could have a crippling effect. The rule for poets seems to be that they will use a rule, knowing that it can be broken or abandoned when necessary. The best judge, in the end, is the ear, not a book on metrics.

IMAGE: in literature an image is a picture in words, and similes, metaphors and
symbols all offer the reader word-pictures as in

> 'his brown skin hung in strips
> like ancient wallpaper,
> and its pattern of darker brown
> was like wallpaper:
> shapes like full-blown roses . . . '
> – Elizabeth Bishop 'The Fish'

> ' . . . where the ocean
> Like a mighty animal
> With a really wicked motion
> Leaps for sailor's funeral . . . '
> – Stevie Smith 'Deeply Morbid'

Ezra Pound defined the image as 'an intellectual and emotional complex in an instant of time' and this definition reminds us that the image involves the head and the heart. Our intellect creates the picture and our emotions are also involved in determining our response to it, and all of this takes place in an instant of time. Single words such as 'snow', 'rat', 'velvet', 'isolation' and so on present us with images of our own making. The poet, in creating a successful image, allows the reader to see something in a new and interesting way.

IMAGERY: the pictures presented in a work of literature which communicate more fully the writer's intention. For example, the predominant imagery in a play by Shakespeare may be light and darkness and these images become powerful ways of portraying characters, moods, the play's structure.

INTERNAL RHYME: this is a rhyme which occurs within the line to create a musical or rhythmical effect, as in Elizabeth Bishop's 'Filling Station', where 'taboret' (American pronunciation) and 'set' and the repeated color form an internal rhyme:

> Some comic books provide
> the only note of *color* —
> of certain *color*. They lie
> upon a big dim doily
> draping a tabor**et**
> (part of the s**et**), beside
> a big hirsute begonia.

IRONY: there are two kinds of irony: verbal irony, when something is said and the opposite is meant; and irony of situation, the classic example being the story of Oedipus.

METAPHOR: when a direct link is made between two things without using 'like' or 'as'. Metaphors are often more powerful than similes. 'You're an angel' is more effective than 'You're like an angel'; 'He blazed a trail through the town' is a metaphor which gives a vivid image of a person directly compared to fire – colourful, exciting, dangerous.

MOOD: this is the feeling contained within a poem and the feeling communicated to the reader. If someone walked into a room containing several people and angrily shouted at you to 'Get out of here at once!' the TONE of voice used would be an ANGRY, COMMANDING one and the MOOD within the room might be one of UNEASE. Do not confuse TONE and MOOD. Tone has to do with the expressing of an attitude; mood has to do with feeling.

NOSTALGIA: a longing for something in the past.

OCTAVE / OCTET: an eight-line stanza. In a Petrarchan sonnet the fourteen lines are divided into octet and sestet. The octet often poses a question and this is answered in the sestet.

ODE: a poem of celebration and praise. John Keats wrote some of the most famous odes in the English Language.

ONOMATOPOEIA: in Greek 'onomatopoeia' means 'the making of a name' and onomatopoeia refers to words whose sounds imitate what is being described. For example, 'buzz', 'slap', 'cuckoo', 'gargle'.

PALINDROME: in Greek the word palindrome means 'running back again'. A palindrome is a word, a line of verse or a sentence which reads the same way backwards and forwards: e.g. 'Dad'; 'noon'; 'Madam, I'm Adam'; 'Was it a cat I saw?'. The following refers to Napoleon: 'Able was I ere I saw Elba'. Other examples are: 'Sums are not set as a test on Erasmus'; and 'A man, a plan, a canal – Panama!'

PARADOX: a paradox is when language expresses a truth in what seems, at first, to be a contradiction. For example, Wordsworth's 'The child is father of the man' or Shakespeare's line in Julius Caesar: 'Cowards die many times before their deaths'.

PARODY: this is when a well-known work is deliberately imitated in a mocking or humorous way. The reader is expected to be familiar with the original work, if the parody is to be effective.

PATHETIC FALLACY: this term was coined by John Ruskin in 1856 and it refers to the writer's technique of attributing human feeling or behaviour to nature. For example, in 'Lycidas' John Milton says of the flowers 'And Daffadillies fill their cups with tears'.

PATHOS: the word pathos in Greek means 'suffering' or 'passion'. Pathos is a deep, sympathetic feeling which the writer summons up in the reader or audience. The final line of Seamus Heaney's poem, 'Mid-term Break' is an example: 'A four foot box, a foot for every year.'

PENTAMETER: This is a line of poetry which is made up of five metrical feet. The iambic pentameter ($\smile - / \smile - / \smile - / \smile - / \smile -$) is the most commonly used meter in the English language.

PERSONA: In Latin the word persona means person or mask, and the persona is the speaker in a work such as poem or play who is different from the poet or playwright. The list of characters in a play used to be given under the heading Dramatis Personae (the dramatist's persons). In Michael Longley's poem 'Self-Heal' and 'Wedding-Wind' by Philip Larkin the voice is that of a female persona.

PERSONIFICATION: this occurs when a writer gives human qualities to animate, inanimate objects or abstractions. For example, if one said that the clouds were in a rage that would be personification.

PUNCTUATION: In Latin the word *punctus* means 'to point' and punctuation indicates speed, flow, emphasis, direction, the emotional charge of language and so on. The following are the more familiar forms:

comma	,	a slight pause
semicolon	;	a longer pause or a division between clauses
colon	:	a long pause; introduces a list, explanation or quotation

full-stop	.	indicates a full stop at the end of a sentence; also used at the end of certain abbreviated words (e.g. Prof. and ad. but not Mr because Mr in the abbreviated version ends with the same letter as the word in full does)
ellipsis	...	indicates that something is missing or is being omitted
dash	–	used to indicate a break in a sentence or elsewhere
hyphen	-	connects compound words
quotation marks	' '	are used to indicate quoted material
	" "	indicate a quotation within a quotation or something of a false or spurious nature
slash	/	indicates a line ending
exclamation mark	!	used for emphasis or to express emotion
question mark	?	suggests puzzlement, confusion, a need for information
parentheses	( )	used in an aside
brackets	[ ]	indicates an editorial comment
italics	*italics*	used for emphasis, foreign words

PUN: a play upon words alike or nearly alike in sound, but different in meaning. A famous example is the dying Mercutio's line in *Romeo and Juliet* (III i): 'Ask for me tomorrow and you shall find me a grave man.'

QUATRAIN: in French 'quatrain' means a collection of four, and quatrain, in English, refers to a poem or stanza of four lines, usually with alternating rhyming schemes such as abab, aabb, abba, aaba, abcb.

REPETITION: repeated sounds, words, structures is a feature of all poetry to a lesser or greater degree. Repetition has many effects such as emphasis, music, surprise, predictability. Paul Durcan's use of repetition in 'Going Home to Mayo, Winter, 1949' or Elizabeth Bishop's use of repetition in the closing lines of 'The Fish' are significant and effective.

RHYME: when a sound is echoed creating a music and order within the work.

RHYTHM: the work in Greek means 'flowing'. Rhythm refers to how the words move or flow.

ROMANTICISM: Romanticism and the Romantic Movement belong to a period in English Literature in the late eighteenth century and the beginning of the nineteenth. Some date the beginning of the movement from the beginning of the French Revolution in 1789; others from 1798 when Wordsworth and Coleridge published *Lyrical Ballads*. The movement ended in the 1830s [Victoria became Queen in 1837]. The movement began as a reaction to the formality and restraint of neo-classicism in the preceding age. The Romantic Movement focused on the individual's feelings and imagination. The child was valued for its innocence and society was regarded as a corrupting influence. The Romantic poet wrote about his own thoughts and feelings [Wordsworth, speaking of The Prelude, said that 'it was a thing unprecedented in literary history that a man should talk so much about himself] and celebrated nature over city life and civilisation. Samuel Johnson, in the eighteenth century, had said that 'The man who is tired of London is tired of life'; the Romantics often found their inspiration in nature.

SARCASM: not to be confused with IRONY, sarcasm is a crude and obvious method of expressing apparent praise when the opposite is meant.

SENSIBILITY: the sensitivity and quality of a person's mind, the capacity of feeling or emotion.

SENSUOUSNESS: a type of writing in which sense descriptions predominate – sight, sound, hearing, smell and taste. Keats's 'To Autumn' is a famous example of sensuous writing.

SENTIMENTALITY: an expression of feeling which is excessive, indulgent, immature.

SESTET: a group of six lines, usually the final six lines in a sonnet where the fourteen line poem is divided into eight (octet) and sestet.

SIMILE: from the Latin word for 'like', the simile is a figure of speech in which one thing is compared to another, using the words 'like', 'as', 'as if'. For example

> When I was small I swallowed an awn of rye.
> My throat was like standing crop probed by a scythe.
> – Seamus Heaney 'The Butter-Print'

SONNET: a fourteen line poem, usually in iambic pentameter.

STREAM OF CONSCIOUSNESS: the phrase was invented by the nineteenth-century American psychologist William James to describe the writer's attempt to imitate or capture every thought, impression, memory, feeling and so on in an individual consciousness, as they happen. The most famous example of stream of consciousness is found in the closing forty pages of James Joyce's *Ulysses*. Here Joyce has entered into Molly Bloom's consciousness. Her thoughts and ideas flow through the reader's mind, and Joyce abandoned all conventional punctuation to give the passage immediacy. Here is an excerpt:

> I love flowers Id love to have the whole place swimming in roses God of heaven theres nothing like nature the wild mountains then the sea and the waves rushing then the beautiful country with fields of oats and wheat and all kinds of things and all the fine cattle going about that would do your heart good to see rivers and lakes and flowers all sorts of shapes and smells and colours springing up even out of the ditches primroses and violets nature it is as for them saying theres no God I wouldnt give a snap of my two fingers for all their learning why dont they go and create something I often asked him atheists or whatever they call themselves go and

wash the cobbles off themselves first then they go howling for the priest and they dying and why why because theyre afraid of hell on account of their bad conscience ah yes I know them well who was the first person in the universe before there was anybody that made it all who ah that they dont know neither do I so there you are they might as well try to stop the sun from rising tomorrow the sun shines for you he said the day we were lying among the rhododendrons on Howth head in the grey tweed suit and his straw hat the day I got him to propose to me yes first I gave him the bit of seedcake out of my mouth and it was leapyear like now yes 16 years ago my God after that long kiss I near lost my breath . . . . .

STYLE: the manner of writing or speaking, e.g. the way a writer uses words may be direct or convoluted or vague or inaccurate or florid . . . . 'Style most shows a man, speak that I may see thee' (Ben Jonson)

SUBJECT MATTER: this refers to the actual material spoken of in the work. For example, a poet may write about a cluttered room which is the subject matter of the poem, but the theme of the poem could be the confusion felt because a relationship has ended. In Elizabeth Bishop's poem 'Filling Station' the subject matter is an oily, dirty, petrol (gas) station but the poem's theme is human endeavour, dignity, love.

SUBLIME: in Latin this means high, lofty, elevated. The sublime in literature refers to moments of heightened awareness, intense feeling. The closing lines of James Wright's poem 'A Blessing' are sublime.

SYMBOL: a symbol is a word, phrase or image which represents something literal and concrete, but also suggests another source of reference. In everyday life a piece of coloured cloth is just that, but that same cloth can be a country's flag. It is both object and symbol. Similarly in literature: in Shakespeare the King is a male character, but he is also the symbol of power, authority and God's presence on earth. The use of symbol is a powerful device because of its rich, complex associative qualities. In Michael Longley's poem 'The Civil Servant' the smashing of the piano is a symbolic act.

SYNECDOCHE: this is a figure of speech in which a part stands for the whole. For example, 'sail' stands for ship; 'hired hands' or 'all hands on deck' means hired persons.

THEME: theme comes from a Greek word meaning 'proposition', and the theme of a work is the main or central idea within the work. Theme should be distinguished from subject matter. For example, the subject matter of Philip Larkin's 'Church Going' is visiting churches, but the theme of the poem is our natural fascination with religion, its power, its effect and its future.

TONE: the tone is the attitude conveyed by the writer. From the writer's tone of voice the reader can identify the attitude of the writer towards his/her subject matter and/or audience. A tone can be reverent, angry, disrespectful, cautious, dismissive, gentle, reserved, slangy, serious.

VERSE: verse comes from the Latin word 'to turn' or 'a line or row of writing'. Verse can now refer to a line in a poem, a stanza, a refrain or a passage from the Bible. Verse can also refer to an entire poem based on regular meter or a poem which is lacking in profundity.

VOICE: this is the distinctive utterance of a writer; it is the sounds we hear when we read or listen to the poem. In other words, a writer's ability to use words in such a way that a reader can recognise that writer's unique quality.

T. S. Eliot identified three voices in poetry:

1. the poet in silent meditation
2. the poet addressing an audience
3. the voice of a dramatic character or persona created by the poet

Acknowledgements

The publishers would like to thank the following for permission to reproduce copyright material in this book.

Poems

"The Uncle Speaks in the Drawing Room", from *Collected Early Poems*: 1950-1970 by Adrienne Rich. Copyright © 1993 by Adrienne Rich. Copyright © 1967,1963, 1962, 1961, 1960, 1959, 1958, 1957, 1956, 1955, 1954, 1953, 1952, 1951 by Adrienne Rich. Copyright © 1984, 1975, 1971, 1969, 1966 by W.W. Norton & Company, Inc. "Aunt Jennifer's Tigers". The lines from "Delta" from *The Fact of a Doorframe: Selected Poems 1950-2001* by Adrienne Rich. Copyright 2002 by Adrienne Rich. Copyright © 2001, 1999, 1995, 1991, 1989, 1986, 1984, 1981, 1967, 1963, 1962, 1961, 1960, 1959, 1958, 1957, 1956, 1955, 1954, 1953, 1952, 1951 by Adrienne Rich. Copyright © 1978, 1975, 1973, 1971, 1969, 1966 by W.W. Norton & Company, Inc. Used by permission of the author and W.W. Norton & Company Inc.

"Filling Station", "The Fish" and "The Prodigal" from *The Complete Poems* 1927-1979 by Elizabeth Bishop. Copyright © 1979, 1983 by Alice Helen Methfessel. Reprinted by permission of Farrar, Straus & Giroux, Inc.

Faber and Faber for "Poppies in July", "The Arrival of the Bee Box" and "Child" from *Collected Poems* by Sylvia Plath.

The Gallery Press for "Grandfather", "After the Titanic" and "Antartctica' from *Collected Poems* (1990) by Derek Mahon; also for "Madly Singing in the City" by Peter Sirr from *Being Everything* (2000); also for "Chronicle" by David Wheatley from *Misery Hill* (2000); also for "Daniel's Duck" from *The Sky Didn't Fall* (2003) by Kerry Hardie.

The Carcanet Press Limited for "Thinking of Mr D" and "Mirror in February", by Thomas Kinsella; also for "The Red Wheelbarrow" from *Collected Poems* by William Carlos Williams.

Faber and Faber for "Anseo" by Paul Muldoon.

Bloodaxe Books Ltd for "For Heidi with Blue Hair" from *The Incident Book* (1986) by Fleur Adcock; also for "Problems" from *Tell Me this is Normal* (2007) by Julie O'Callaghan; also for "Jungian Cows" by Penelope Shuttle; also for "Night Drive" from *Familiar Strangers: New and Selected Poems* 1960-2004 by Brendan Kennelly.

Photographs